MY KID LEADS!

A How-To Book for Parents Wanting to Raise Future Leaders Today

Plus a Free Leadership Aptitude Assessment

ALAN E. NELSON, Ed.D.

Alan E Nelson, EdD

ISBN: 9781089709855

Summit Publishing

235A N Moorpark Dr., Ste. 1622

Thousand Oaks, CA 91358

Dedication & Thanks

This book is dedicated to our three sons, their kids, and parents around the world interested in developing their child's leadership potential.

Thanks to Jeff White for his graphic design and advice.

Thanks to Andrea Zimmerman and Thayer Riley, for their editing.

And as always, thanks to Nancy, my wife of nearly 40 years, who has put up with me for nearly 2/3 of her life.

Table of Contents

NOTE: *For years, I (the author) taught a graduate course at the University of Southern California titled Human Capital Performance and Motivation. The word "motivation" is from a Latin derivative meaning "to move." Feel free to be childlike in reading this book, letting your curiosity move you to whatever chapter seems the most interesting in the moment. Don't let the chapter numbers confine you.*

A Message from the Author

For over quarter of a century, I've been writing books and teaching classes on leadership and related topics. But I've never written a more important book than the one you're holding right now. At midlife, I came to the conclusion that we were wasting our best leadership content by using it too late. We needed to get to leaders while they're moldable, not moldy. That's why we created KidLead and our project-based training curricula, LeadYoung Training Systems.

I'm impressed that you'd pick up this book to learn how you can develop your child's leadership potential. As a pioneer in this field, I realize that most people who specialize in leadership work with adults and those who work with children usually never focus on leadership studies. Thus, I've been striving to build a bridge between these two areas since midlife.

Regardless of your child's aptitude for leading, I'm jazzed that you're intrigued about the idea of developing his or her leadership potential. This book is filled with practical ideas that will help you do just that. Feel free to skip around the chapters as you like. Let your curiosity steer you. My partners in China, who are developing KidLead there, asked me to do a series of 44 podcasts. After doing that, I decided to share this with everyone.

Imagine time travel, where leaders come to us from the future, for development. In a way, that's what you're doing with our kids, raising leaders from the future. I'm excited to share practical ideas with you that I've learned over the last 15 years, after interacting with thousands of students around the world, focusing on organizational leadership training. Although I continue to teach leadership and organizational behavior in top-tier universities, my heart yearns to develop leaders from the future. That's where you come into the picture, because parents and educators are best positioned to identify leadership giftedness early. Use this book as a resource to develop your leader from the future. If you do this, you'll be able to say with pride and authenticity, "My Kid Leads!"

Alan E. Nelson, EdD

Los Angeles, California

Chapter 1

Why You Should Read This Book

Theme: Four benefits of reading this book.

This is a picture of our three sons when they were very young (Jeff, Jesse, and Josh). They're now grown, responsible, self-actualized men. But in the minds of my wife and myself, it was only yesterday when we held them in our arms, played baseball on the front lawn, and tucked them into bed with a story and prayer. When your kids are young, you have the feeling that life as you know it now will linger for a long time, but it doesn't. What you do now to help them prepare for adulthood is essential.

I teach organizational behavior, leadership, and human capital performance and motivation at USC Marshall School of Business, the Naval Postgraduate School, and the University of California Irvine. These are all top schools, attracting some of the brightest students from around the world. But unlike most people who've earned a doctorate in leadership and work with adults in business, for the last 10-15 years I've studied how to identify and develop leaders at a young age. And when I say young, I mean very young, as early as ages 2 & 3.

Crazy as it sounds, you can often identify who is going to be a leader in preschool. Imagine what it could mean to our schools, organizations, and society at large if we began developing leadership talent at a very young age, as we sometimes do with our athletes, artists, and academicians. If you have children, you're obviously busy, so let me give you four reasons savvy parents should read this book.

1. *Feed to succeed*: I want to help you set up your child to succeed. Although this isn't specifically a book on parenting, it may help your child get into top-tier universities. As I mentioned, I'm fortunate to teach at USC Marshall School of Business, a top 10 undergrad program and top 25 grad school. Who wouldn't want their child to attend a great university if they could? Yet I see a trend among many parents who solely emphasize academics. While I can't question parental motives, I see how many have failed to keep up with the way top colleges accept their students. A while ago I interviewed admissions staff members from Harvard, MIT, Duke, Stanford, and of course, USC. Stanford only accepts approximately 8% of applicants and USC Marshall just under 18%. That's a lot of disappointment for some really smart, hardworking families. What admissions counselors are looking for today, even more than high GPA and SAT scores, are well-rounded students.

   A Stanford admissions staff member said, "We know that most of the people who apply to Stanford could get a degree here, but we're also interested in what students can do for us while they're here. We want to know they are going to make an impact with their lives. We turn away valedictorians and perfect

SAT scores every year. The parents are dumbfounded, because they invested in tutors and made sure their students took all the AP classes available. But in addition to strong grades, we want to see things like service and leadership." In the United States, we invest billions of dollars in youth athletics, even though less than one tenth of one percent will ever play the sport past high school. So why not invest in a life skill that we can literally use all our lives, in addition to making a good income?

2. *Lift the gift*: A second benefit of this book is to help you learn the early indicators of leadership giftedness. If these are present, you'll want to develop your young leader early. Research shows that those in leadership roles enjoy their work more, get paid more, and feel more confident about themselves. Naturally, everyone isn't going to be a leader, organizationally speaking. But how do you know if your child is wired to lead? We've learned what these early indicators are, so while we can't and won't tell you if your child will never ever lead, we can tell you if they can learn leadership skills before others. We've learned that adults often confuse leadership with other things, so they overlook budding CEOs and managers. Thus, you'll discover if you should invest more time and energy in this area or just cross it off your list and look for other aptitudes.

3. *Start smart*: A third benefit of this book is offering your child a head start in terms of his or her leadership development. Harvard published the results of a survey of 17,000 managers, asking when they experienced their first formal leadership training. The average answer: 42. FORTY-TWO! That's long past the time we're pliable in our character and elevated in our cognitions. Therefore, you'd be giving your child a 20- to 30-year head start. In his book *Outliers*, Malcolm Gladwell notes that one of the things highly successful people have over others is a significantly greater amount of experience in a specialized task or field. Since high-level leading today is more complicated than it's ever been, you'll be setting up your child to rise above the rest in their field.

4. *Lessen the stressin'*:A fourth benefit of this book may be more for you than your child. We'll offer you practical ideas on how to raise a strong leader. You can't raise young leaders the same as other children. It's not that they're better than others, but they are different from non-leader children. A lot of parents get frustrated and feel like they're doing a lousy job as a parent, simply because they're not using the proper skills and techniques required for kids with a high leadership aptitude. Plus you'll be able to educate friends, family members, coaches, and teachers on more effective ways to develop young leaders, who are sometimes perceived to be strong-willed, difficult to restrain, outspoken, and even rebellious by those lacking the right skill set. So if nothing else, this book may save you a lot of headaches, not to mention strained parent-child relations.

While this book may not be for every parent, it has the ability to change the lives of many. All good parents love their kids and want the best for them. Yet all kids are not the same. My wife and I have three sons, all of whom are healthy, vibrant, productive adults. Our oldest has a graduate degree from Duke University and now works there. Our middle son has an MBA and a master's degree in real estate development from USC. Our youngest recently finished his degree, has been a strength and conditioning trainer for the LA Dodgers farm team, and is now a physiologist for the Four Seasons Hotel. They're all ambitious and successful, and they're also all very different. If we treated them the same, we'd have been ineffective as parents, because they're not the same. You need to treat each child uniquely to how they're wired. Parenting style needs to match the child, just like shoes should fit their feet.

Bravo to you for taking an interest in developing your child and potentially raising one of the most dynamic leaders we've seen. I will share with you some of the leading insights and best practices in this unique field of young leader development.

Chapter 2

Defining Leadership

Theme: Defining what we mean about leadership, leader, and leading is important for understanding what's required to lead.

In the children's book "Alice's Adventure in Wonderland," Alice has an interesting conversation with the Cheshire Cat. She says, "Would you tell me, please, which way I ought to go from here?"

"That depends a good deal on where you want to get to," said the Cat.

"I don't much care where," said Alice.

"Then it doesn't matter which way you go," said the Cat.

"... so long as I get somewhere," Alice added as an explanation.

"Oh, you're sure to do that," said the Cat, "if you only walk long enough."

Now that we've launched this book and before I offer you 42 more chapters on developing your child's leadership ability, I need to invest a few moments with you, clarifying what is unique about leadership training and even what we mean by *leadership*. Otherwise you may end up like Alice in Wonderland, walking around without having a destination in mind. I've been a student of leadership my entire life. I was a leader in school, where I sometimes got in trouble for it. I was a leader in college. My wife worked for John Maxwell, one of the top leadership authors and trainers in the world, and I made it a point to be around him as much as I could. So when I wanted to get a doctorate, it was only natural that I focused on leadership studies. In fact, I earned my degree from the first university to offer a doctorate in the field, the University of San Diego.

But the interesting thing about leadership is that it's a relatively new field of study. In fact, the word *leadership* doesn't occur in the English language until 1821. We've always been interested in leaders and how they lead, but official study and research in the field of leadership did not begin until the 1940s. Another interesting thing is that of my 700 books on leadership, less than 5% define the term. So it seems that everyone likes to talk about leadership, but few clarify what they mean. Since we're going to be talking a lot about leadership in this series, let me define what we're discussing.

Leadership is the process of helping people accomplish together what they would not or could not as individuals. **Leaders** are individuals who catalyze this social process. And **leading** is how they do it. So while I don't want to get into a debate about defining leadership, I want you to know that I see it differently than many others who refer to leadership, at least in the United States and Western society. Because leadership is such a popular term, many use it to refer to anything related to achievement and personal growth. It sells well, but this is non-productive because when you specifically want to discuss organizational leadership or what a leader does to lead a team of people, we confuse it with any number of other things.

If you get in a conversation with others about leadership, I'd encourage you to ask them to define what they mean. I've discovered that when people who work with children and youth talk about leadership, they're typically referring to things like self-actualization, self-esteem, confidence, character, service, citizenship, and self-efficacy. These are all important and wonderful qualities, but they are different from leading people. This is not the leadership we teach in our MBA classes or executive education. So if we want to raise effective and ethical leaders by getting to them while they're moldable, we should use a definition of leadership that is applicable for them in the future. Therefore, for the sake of this book, we're going to be talking about a much narrower definition—and thus, it is unique. If you want to develop your child's leadership potential so that he or she will be taken seriously as a leader, not just a good employee or team member, you'll need to understand what is unique about leading vs. non-leading.

No doubt, you're learning new skills as a parent that you did not have before you started raising children. Your child will also be learning new skills as a young person. Some of these involve reading and writing and academics. You also probably enroll your child in programs such as sports and athletics, as well as art and music. People who train children in these skills use certain methods and techniques that are unique to each skill. For example, you don't use the same approach to teach a child math that you do to teach how to kick a soccer ball or play a piano. The methods need to match the desired skill set. The same is true of leadership.

Another interesting thing we've discovered in looking at leaders when they're very young is that nearly all organizational leadership assessments focus on improving effectiveness, not identifying emergence. There are dozens and dozens of surveys and instruments designed to help adult leaders get better. Yet because children and youth have little experience in formal leadership roles, these surveys and assessments don't help us a lot. We want to find out who is more likely to emerge as a leader, not just get better at leading. Let me give you an example.

We want leaders who can communicate well and who possess the ability to convey their thoughts and ideas in articulate ways that others understand. Plus we want them to have other people skills such as respect for others, good conflict management, and effective listening. But think about it, we also want those same skills in our team members, people who aren't necessarily ever going to lead a team. We want team members who communicate well, honor others, manage conflict, and listen. These qualities are what we refer to as Type 2 leader qualities, characteristics we want in leaders as well as people who don't lead. When you observe a good leader, you're apt to see these characteristics, but these don't make the person a leader, just a better one.

So what is unique to leading? What are the qualities required to emerge as a leader, not just to be better at leading? These are what we categorize as Type 1 qualities, those that are unique to leading. The four aptitudes that we introduce in Chapter 6 are unique to leading, as long as they are in combination with each other. These have to do with the ability to persuade, the ability to develop a plan, comfort and willingness in handling power, and being propelled and self-motivated to initiate things. When combined, these four qualities help us identify who is most likely to emerge as a leader, whether you're an adult working in a large corporation or a preschooler recruiting your peers to a playground game.

Because our goal determines how we accomplish it, it is important for us to have a clear definition of leadership when we're working with little kids or teenagers. People who say they are teaching young people how to lead, but only focus on service, citizenship, self-esteem, character, and confidence, are more than likely building strong people, but not necessarily people who understand how to lead. That's because leadership is a unique ability, just as math is different from spelling and playing a violin is different from dribbling a basketball. If we want to bring out the leadership potential in a child, we need to have a clear idea of what that is. It helps us know when we have done a good job training a child and when we have not. So moving forward, remember that the concept of leadership we're discussing in this book is the process of helping people accomplish together what they would not or could not as individuals. Leaders are those who get this social process going and leading is how they do it. That makes leadership training unique from other activities.

Chapter 3

Your Child's Success in the AI Era

Theme: Why leadership has a significant impact on a child's lifelong growth.

This is truly an exciting time to live and an even more amazing time to be raising kids. The world is changing fast. We're living in a time when the future looks bright yet also very difficult to predict because of the rapid rate of change. I live near Malibu, California. Often I'll go to the ocean and watch the surfers on Surfrider beach trying to maneuver big waves when the surf is up. Surfing is a good metaphor when thinking about managing the future, because the waves are dynamic and changing. But with practice and an eye on the waves, I'm confident you can do that. One of the biggest disruptors to our lives is technological improvements.

An emerging frontier a lot of people are talking about is artificial intelligence, where software programs can potentially take over entire industries that currently require masses of people. Every day, I interact with one of my three Amazon "Alexa," an artificial intelligence device that provides access to news, weather, interesting facts, a joke, online ordering, shopping lists, and ocean sounds for sleeping. In the United States, it's estimated that self-driving trucks will take the place of over half the long-haul drivers by 2040. Obviously, as concerned parents, we want to prepare your child to avoid being replaced by a computer, app, or robot. Futurists are predicting what the next 10-25 years will be like in terms of which professions are most likely and least likely to be replaced by technology. A study published by Oxford University estimated that the role of CEO was one of the lowest to be impacted, rating it at only 1.5%. Even then, much of this minor risk is a matter of task versus role, in that leaders will have better access to information and risk assessment, thus aiding them in deciding more effectively and efficiently.

Traditionally, parents have wanted to help their child or children get into professions such as law and medicine, believing these roles to be at the top of the food chain. Ironically, both law and medicine are quickly being subsidized with AI, or computers and robotics. More and more companies are outsourcing activities in these fields to lower income segments, thanks to technology and the ability to create solutions at a far lower cost. But while some of the legendary blue-chip professions are being replaced by progress such as artificial intelligence, people-oriented roles and professions are perceived to be in higher demand in the future.

Leaders deal with humans and help them adapt to changes. As long as people inhabit the earth, we'll need those who organize us and help us accomplish together what we would not or could not as individuals. The process of creating synergy, whereby the total outcome is greater than the sum of the individual parts, is what leaders do best. Plus, as leading grows in complexity, we will need to come up with new ways of identifying leadership talent at a much earlier age, because it will take more time to develop a more sophisticated leader. As we seek more and better leaders, we'll need to start younger.

Since 2006, my primary work has involved adapting what we know about organizational leadership to the very, very young. To the best of my knowledge, I've done more work in this field than anyone in the world, reviewing the literature and research and interacting with over 15,000 children and youth internationally. I've created a robust assessment and project-based training curricula. And yet, while people are interested in the latest app to order food or connect with friends, we seem to be satisfied with archaic ways of selecting leaders. It seems we'd rather complain about the leaders we have than design new ways to identify them early and develop them over the long haul.

Traditionally, throughout history, we've let leaders sort of percolate up on their own, bubbling to the surface and then hoping they'll be both ethical and effective. Although technology, such as the internet, GPS, genetic engineering, AI, and the global village have changed society, we're still in the Middle Ages when it comes to identifying and developing leaders. I'd like to say we've discovered a way to turn any child into a future CEO, but we haven't. The plethora of research behind positive psychology shows that we're most apt to succeed in the areas of our strengths. As someone said, "A child is a book to be read, not to be written." Therefore, as responsible parents, our job is to figure out how our children are wired and then help them focus on these aptitudes and potential early, giving them a huge head start.

So the bad news is that everyone isn't going to become a great leader, just like you can't turn all kids into NBA players like LeBron James. But the good news is that we've learned how to identify children with leadership gifts and we've pioneered a way to develop them as leaders, with organizational leadership skills. I believe we are on the fringe of a truly exciting social movement that will allow us to develop our best leadership talent in history, through an intentional and methodological system.

Our goal at KidLead is to get to leaders while they're moldable, not moldy. We want to make the world a better place, and we need the help of parents like you to look for the early indicators of leadership aptitude and then develop them early while they're malleable.

Sometimes, when I'm doing a workshop, I end by showing a photo of Usain Bolt, a Jamaican who is currently the fastest man in the world, running 100 meters in 9.58 seconds. I say to my audience, "I'll bet you $100 that I can beat this man in a race." People smile, as they look at my aging, less athletic physique. Then I grin back at them and say, "I can beat this man in a race as long as you give me a big enough head start." So if you want to give your child a 20- to 30-year head start on learning how to lead, you've come to the right place.

Think about it, every great leader throughout history was at one time a preschooler, a preteen, and then a teen. What did they act like? How were they different from their peers? What caused them to rise to the top of the influence pile? So while I'm a fan of any adult who develops the potential in a child, I'm exceptionally grateful for those interested in young leader development, because leaders are the ones who make history, not the masses. Leaders help us all accomplish more together than we can alone.

In a world experiencing so many rapid changes, making jobs of the future unstable and unsure, we'll always need those who know how to organize people and help them adapt and adjust to these transitions. We need organizational and cultural surfers who know how to ride the waves of change. That's what leaders do.

Chapter 4

Ready to Raise a Leader?

Theme: Parents need to intentionally consider if they want to develop their child's leadership potential.

I remember when we were raising our children and we'd play Hide and Seek. Everyone went to hide except for the person who was the seeker. The finder had to close his eyes and count loudly so the others could hear. Then he'd say, "Ready or not, here I come." And no matter how planned or unplanned your children were, ready or not, they came. When my wife and I were preparing for our three sons, we read books, talked to others, and had many discussions on how we wanted to raise them. We painted their rooms, purchased new furniture, and tried to create a warm and inviting place for them to live. Now as grandparents, we see our kids doing the same for their children.

So just as you are intentional in how you parent your children, you'll need to be intentional if you want to raise a young leader. Here are four practical things to consider if you want to develop their leadership potential effectively.

First, young leader development begins between your ears. That's right, it doesn't begin with the child. What you think about leadership, and more importantly, how you think about your child in terms of leadership will significantly impact how your child responds. There's a story in Greek mythology called the Pygmalion. It's the story of an artist who sculpts a beautiful statue of a woman. Pygmalion then fell in love with his own statue. The goddess of love noticed his affection and decided to turn the sculpture into a real woman, so the artist and his new love could live happily ever after together. The Pygmalion Effect is that people tend to become as they're treated. So if you start thinking of your child as a leader, you'll start treating them that way. This will help the child to see himself or herself as a leader and start behaving that way.

A second thing to consider, if you're ready to raise a young leader, is how you need to treat your child uniquely. Obviously, if you have only one child, this may not be as applicable, but if you have more than one, you'll quickly see their differences. We have three sons. Our oldest and youngest were compliant, meaning that when we needed to correct them, a simple verbal warning was pretty much all they required. But our middle son, who possesses the highest natural leadership aptitude, was very strong willed and typically non-compliant. Therefore, we needed to parent him differently. If we had parented our middle son the same as his brothers, we would not have equipped him with the skills he needed to succeed in life. Conversely, if we parented our oldest and youngest the same as our middle son, we would have discouraged them and not helped them succeed. Children with high leadership aptitude are different from their siblings and most other kids.

Therefore, to be equitable, you can't treat them equally. You'll need to adjust and customize the way you parent, such as disciplining, challenging, communicating, and training. We'll talk more about this in upcoming chapters.

A third thing to do is to compare your leadership aptitude with your child's. We'll talk more about measuring your child's natural talent in another chapter, but here's a quick way to compare you and your child's wiring. If you're a strong leader and your child seems to possess lower leadership ability, you'll want to avoid these two common problems. One is when a parent is overbearing, trying to take charge and thus intimidate the child. This is what I experienced with my father. I was a leader, but my dad considered my leadership behavior as rebelliousness. He quickly shut it down, conveying the idea that there was only room for one leader in the family; naturally, him. Thus whenever I was around my dad, I was quiet and wore a mask of passivity, to avoid conflict. This is common among strong leader parents, who shut down their child's leadership potential, well-intended or not. Our partners in Thailand informed us that this is common in Asian cultures where children are often taught to be quiet around adults, confusing reserved behavior with respect.

The other problem we've discovered is when strong leader parents want their child to be something they aren't. Forcing a non-leader child into leadership roles is a great way to set up your child for discouragement and failure. When our sons were young, I coached many of their athletic teams. I interacted with numerous parents who thought their child was going to be the next great professional baseball, soccer, or basketball player. The problem is that most kids will never reach this level of play. Yet the parents behaved badly, putting pressure on the child to do things that he or she was unable to do. This transcends the Pygmalion concept, causing children to resent their parents and end up hating the activities designed for fun and recreation.

Those are two things to consider if your leadership ability is greater than your child's. But what if you realize your child may have stronger leadership aptitude than you? Here are two different things you'll want to consider. First, do you perceive your child's strong will and non-compliance as rebelliousness? As a person who isn't strong in leading, you may be projecting a perception to your child that he or she is a troublemaker. Thus the Pygmalion Effect will be working against your child. There's a difference between a disrespectful child and one who's merely trying to do what comes naturally to him as a leader. Another concern when a child possesses more leadership aptitude than the parent is a lack of role modeling and development, in that the parent simply does not know how to train the child in the areas of leading. Again, we'll discuss more practical ideas in future chapters, but being aware of leadership talent differences can prepare you to raise a leader.

A fourth way to prepare for raising your child as a leader is to begin thinking of your home as a leadership *dojo*. The word *dojo* is Japanese and refers to a place of training. In the adult world, we often think of leadership development settings as on-the-job or in academic settings, such as where I teach at USC Marshall School of Business. We also think of it in high-priced retreats, executive coaching, and professionally facilitated programs. But every week, dozens of opportunities arise within the normal day-to-day functions of family life where a child can learn leadership skills. We'll share several ideas in upcoming chapters, but it's time to begin thinking of opportunities for your child to lead family projects and functions, for the primary purpose of developing his or her leadership potential. Remember, young leader training starts between your ears as a parent in how you think about your child, considering your leadership differences and developing leadership training experiences in everyday settings.

Let me end with a little story. In 1969, I was a 10-year-old child. I remember watching Neil Armstrong walk on the moon, on a television with a black and white screen, in our farmhouse in rural Iowa. Over 30 years later, as an adult, I had the opportunity to introduce our three sons to the famous astronaut at a special event we attended. While Neil Armstrong was famous for being the first human on the moon, he didn't wake up one day and say, "I think I'll go to the moon." Countless efforts went into helping him succeed at this task, involving a lot of people and intentional planning. I realize this may be an exaggerated example, but IF you want to develop a great young leader, you'll need to be intentional. It won't just happen. And it will also require involving other people, because leading is primarily a social skill. But if you consider the four things discussed in this chapter, you will be ready to raise a leader from the future.

Chapter 5

Are Leaders Made or Born?

Theme: Research shows that certain children possess a predisposition to lead, but must still be developed.

If you do an internet search on the topic "Are leaders made or born," you'll see that millions of others have asked the same question. Throughout history, most in society have believed that certain people were born to be leaders. These are typically sons and daughters of royalty and certain classes of people. But with the rise of democracy, capitalism, and pop psychology, people frequently say, "You can achieve whatever you want to in life. Anyone can be a leader if they want. Leaders are made, not born." So while I'm a big fan of motivation and human performance, the last 10-15 years of research in the fields of genetics and neuroscience are suggesting that the truth seems to be in the middle of the road, that leaders are both made *and* born.

In 1972, the U.S. Congress commissioned a report of gifted and talented education because it was concerned that other countries were doing a better job of developing exceptional talent than we were. Dr. Marland, then the commissioner of education, presented a report that became known as the Marland Report. It recognized the need to identify kids with exceptional talent in public education. Among the list of gifts recognized was leadership. Even today, the U.S. Department of Education acknowledges leadership as a gift, although little to nothing is done to develop it in schools. In the 1980s, Harvard Professor Howard Gardner wrote a bestselling book on the subject of multiple intelligences. Dr. Gardner listed eight areas of exceptional ability, including language, math, art, kinesthetic, and people smarts. In that last domain, he noted leadership as a subset. When I asked him why he included leadership, he said, "Because when you observe groups of students, you realize that some possess a unique ability to lead others."

What Drs. Marland and Gardner stated in their work involving scores of students is being upheld by those who study genetics. A large database of twins has allowed us to see what becomes of people over a number of years. When you compare identical twins who share nearly 100% of the same DNA and fraternal twins who share approximately 50%, you can see who emerges into roles of authority, leadership, and influence and better understand the differences between genetics and environment. Depending on which leadership traits you focus on, between 10-60% is inherited, meaning that we gain them from birth, much like the color of our eyes, skin, hair, and our IQ.

So although genetics doesn't guarantee a person will or will not become a leader in life, it certainly sets some up to excel more than the rest. We refer to this as predisposition. Consider athletics, perhaps a more common and obvious natural talent. Certain kids, because of their body types, eye-hand coordination, balance, and muscle tone are predisposed toward certain sports, whether gymnastics, basketball, or track and field. While all kids can learn these sports, some possess an innate ability, unlike their peers. Translate this into art. Budding singers, graphic artists, and instrumentalists stand out among their peers at very young ages.

The same is true of leading. A predisposition to lead means that a child will frequently gravitate toward situations where they can practice their leading. At the same time, adults recognize their ability to influence peers, so that they get invited to be project leaders, team captains, and classroom monitors, further developing their raw talent beyond the rest.

Naturally, there's an array of other environmental influences such as culture, parental influence, sibling ability, education, and the role of significant others. For example, parents who are themselves leaders will often talk about leadership situations at work during dinner, introduce their children to other leaders, and pursue opportunities for the child to learn about leading. A sibling who is a strong leader may actually reduce a younger brother or sister's opportunity to lead, because he or she is older. We also notice a significant difference in cultures. In many Asian cultures, children are perceived to be rebellious and disrespectful if they are opinionated and outspoken, so parents strive to reduce their social influence, especially when other adults are present. As we mentioned in the previous chapter, a parent who lacks leadership aptitude will often not know how to develop a child with exceptional leadership ability and thus fail to help the child to develop.

The point of this chapter is that leadership is a unique ability, much like athletic and artistic ability, IQ, and extroversion versus introversion. A child's natural talent creates a predisposition to develop leadership skills or not. So the question is, are leaders made or born? The answer is, "Yes."

I grew up on a farm in the Midwest. We raised cattle, hogs, hay, and corn. One day, when I was 9 or 10, my father and I were standing in the neighbor's soybean field. He pointed to a tall stalk of corn that was much higher than the rest of the soybeans. My dad asked, "Do you know what that is?" I looked at him oddly, because I knew what it was and I knew he knew what it was. I said, "It's corn." My dad said, "It's a weed." I looked at him again. I knew it wasn't a weed, because we had entire fields of corn. "It's a stalk of corn," I repeated. My dad said, "Anything that's not where it's supposed to be is a weed."

Some might suggest that leadership should not be considered in the field of genetic research, but it's not a weed. It's how some kids are wired. They possess a predisposition to organize others, catalyzing them to work together toward a common goal. So while there is no single leadership gene that we've identified, the realm of genetics and neuroscience are showing us that certain qualities have the ability to elevate some to the arena of leading others. While this may not be a fatalistic destiny for some to lead and others never to lead, it does give us an incentive to identify those with these predispositions and then help them develop organizational leadership abilities at a very young age.

Chapter 6

Eight Indicators of Leadership Giftedness

Theme: Eight ways to assess your child's leadership aptitude.

Nearly all assessments on adult development focus on helping existing leaders get better. They look at effectiveness. But when you're looking at leaders before they possess formal opportunities to lead organizationally, you need to look at leadership emergence, meaning who's most apt to emerge as a leader. We've found that this gives us a sense of who can learn leadership at an early age and thus, who it is we want to intentionally develop in terms of leadership skill, giving these young leaders a huge head start.

We have developed an online leadership assessment tool that provides a more robust instrument for estimating the probability of leadership giftedness. The NYLI is for ages 6-18 and the Social Influence Survey is for even younger children. So while I'd encourage you to use these resources, let me give you eight indicators of what we look for in identifying children and youth with high leadership potential, similar to the way a coach would look for a budding athlete or an educator would try to identify an academic prodigy.

We've found four sub-aptitudes consistent among children and youth with a high probability of leadership giftedness. I'll introduce each of these, along with two examples of the more common behaviors observable.

The first is what we call persuasive. Although a child can be persuasive and not a leader, leaders must be able to persuade because they must sell their ideas and themselves to others so that they gain followers.

One skill observable in this category is conveying opinions. That may seem like an odd quality, but leaders have opinions—ideas on how things could be done better, how to fix problems, or ways to accomplish goals. So while everyone with an opinion isn't a leader, leaders possess ideas and want to share them. This can be irritating as an adult, especially for those who believe that children should be "seen and not heard," but it's vital for adults to allow leaders to share their opinions.

Another persuasive behavior is the ability to negotiate with peers and adults, to get their way. This may be something as simple as a school playground suggestion of what to play or pleading the case with a parent of why she or he should be able to stay up later than normal bedtime. This skill is not the same as a child who cries and throws a tantrum. Rather, the negotiator can logically and emotionally motivate others to see his or her viewpoint.

The second aptitude we see in children gifted in leadership is self-motivation. We refer to this as being propelled, meaning that the child exhibits behavior that seems to motivate him or her toward goals. Because leaders are goal-oriented by nature, this makes sense when we see children who like starting things, setting goals, and creating new ventures.

One behavior in this category is that the child can be seen starting new things. For example, when our middle son was in high school, we belonged to an indoor tennis club that offered a Sunday afternoon program for teens. He felt frustrated that they charged money for it but didn't provide any instruction. Therefore, he started his own Sunday afternoon program and charged his friends a modest fee and a can of tennis balls. They used free courts at a local high school. So many teens followed him that the tennis club shut down their Sunday afternoon program. We didn't suggest this to him, but rather he initiated the program on his own. He's done things like this throughout his life.

Another indicator of leadership aptitude in this category is a voluntary drive to get involved in clubs, activities, and projects. Again, while students who express this aren't necessarily leaders, those who are leaders don't seem to need adults to urge them to get more involved. Students who express dreams, goals, and involvement are driven by an inner need to achieve. Leaders are achievers. It's just that they tend to achieve with and through others.

A third aptitude we see in students gifted in leadership is the ability to plan. I don't mean this in the same sense of an engineer or software programmer, but rather those who can both see the big picture and break it down into steps.

One behavior in this category is the ability to think strategically. Strategic thinking sees the end result and then comes up with paths to accomplish the objective. When a person is unable to do both, see the concept and come up with steps, she or he likely doesn't have strong leadership aptitude. Leaders are unique in that they can see the big picture, a right hemisphere brain process, as well as see some of the details, a left hemisphere brain process. The ability to do both is common among leaders.

Another behavior in this category is assigning roles to peers. Naturally, this is an example of seeing the larger objective and then breaking it into tasks. For example, a preschool student may suggest to her peers that they play "school." In the process, the girl assigns herself as the teacher and other students are told where to sit, what to do, and how to behave. If others follow this girl, then she likely possesses this ability. The result is that others comply.

The fourth sub-category of leadership emergence is power. More than the other three, this category is most unique to leaders. A leader must feel comfortable handling power, authority, and influence. A "powerless leader" is an oxymoron. Leaders deal in power and influence.

One behavior common among children with high leadership aptitude is the willingness to assume leadership roles. Often these students will seek these roles, whether in the classroom, on the playground, the neighborhood, or athletic team. You'll see adults select these children for roles of authority because they trust them to be in charge and see their potential to influence peers.

Another behavior is standing up to authority to correct an injustice or correct something that the child believes needs to change. Leaders are change agents. Plus they're more comfortable with power, resulting in their willingness to stand up to a bully, an adult, or another authority figure.

These eight qualities, representing four aptitudes indicative of students who possess high leadership aptitude, offer an insight into children more likely to benefit from leadership development at a very young age. As I mentioned at the start of this chapter, I'd recommend that you do an assessment on your child using the SIS (ages 3-5) or the NYLI (ages 6-18) online instruments. This will help you assess if your child will benefit from more intentional and formal leadership training, regardless of his or her age. You or another adult who has seen the child in social settings should take the assessment on the child. The SIS and NYLI are free and available at www.LeadYoungTraining.com.

Chapter 7

The Optimum Time to Train Leaders

Theme: The "10-13 Window" is the intersection of character pliability and cognitive-social-emotional development.

As I've mentioned previously, I grew up on a farm in the middle of the United States. We raised crops, so every year I'd watch my dad determine when the best time was to plant a crop. A lot of it had to do with the type of crop, the specific hybrid of the seed, and of course weather conditions. The time windows for planting and harvesting were critical to the yield of the crop, meaning how much they'd produce by harvest time.

Humans also have seasons—developmental windows when they are more or less prone to achieve or accomplish certain things related to life matters. So while we applaud any opportunity to work on leadership development, there are strategic times when teaching leadership skills are more effective than others. Traditionally, we've considered leadership an adult trait, so that serious leadership development takes place after employees have proven themselves as leaders and/or risen the corporate ladder sufficiently to justify an investment in formal leadership training.

Our work has shown us when children are most apt to begin benefitting from concentrated skill development. We began developing our training curricula by reviewing the theories and research related to human development, namely three aspects: cognitive, ethical, and socio-emotional. Let me explain the importance of each one.

Cognitive development is an important part of learning how to lead because leaders strategize, plan, and problem solve. Plus students need to receive coaching and feedback, so a certain level of critical thinking is needed. We looked at Piaget and other developmental psychologists in terms of stages. We have noticed a somewhat significant jump around age 10 in terms of critical thinking and the ability to process information, along with communication skills important for giving and receiving information.

Another area we investigated was character development, because our goal was to help develop ethical leaders. History is scarred by unethical leaders, depriving society because of their character. Therefore, we read moral development experts such as Kohlberg to analyze when humans are pliable in their character. This begins very young, as early as 2 years old, when we begin to recognize the difference between right and wrong. Although people can change in their character at all ages, most agree that our compass is primarily established by age 13, after which we're more adult-like in our thinking and behavior. Thus, we stablished 13 as the upper limit for optimum training in this area. So while it's always good to teach ethics, ethics courses in MBA programs aren't going to do much to change students. It's little more than an intellectual discussion.

The third developmental issue we considered was socio-emotional maturity, because leading is primarily a people skill. This has to do with things such as emotional intelligence, the ability for self and others awareness, along with managing our emotions and our interactions with others. Again, in our work with the young and very young leaders, we found that those under the age of 10 demonstrate a more difficult time understanding relational dynamics and working together in teams.

Thus, after laying the developmental stages of cognitions, character, and social emotional maturity on top of each other, we discovered a strategic overlapping between the ages of 10 and 13. That's why we refer to it as the 10-13 Window. This is the prime time to teach organizational leadership skills if we want to focus on both ethics and effectiveness at the same time. The big problem is that people who specialize in leadership nearly always work with adults, and people who specialize with children and youth rarely study leadership. Our goal at KidLead is to build a bridge between leadership expertise and children, getting to leaders while they're young and giving them a big head start.

Although age 10 is the youngest time to incorporate accelerated training methods, we can start much younger in terms of looking for giftedness by allowing children to experience opportunities of working together in task-oriented teams, as well as giving them opportunities to lead peers in projects. This is the purpose behind our preschool and early childhood curricula. These programs give parents, educators, and children's workers the opportunity to see who is most apt to benefit from more concentrated training later. It's a bit like watering and fertilizing a seed to see how it grows.

The 10-13 Window provides an opportunity for us to peek into the future, identifying leaders early. This practice has now been observed in several cultures and countries, involving thousands of students. So while the 10-13 Window represents the bullseye of our target, we're also interested in assisting those who come before and after this developmental stage, offering skills for leading others by using age and stage training methods.

Let me close with another illustration. Probably most of us have played miniature golf, also known as Putt-Putt golf. Many miniature golf courses have one hole that has a large windmill where a door opens and closes. The goal is to hit the ball when the door is closed so that when it gets to it, it will be open. If you hit the ball at the wrong time, it will be blocked and knocked into the water or out of the path to the hole. As a leadership specialist, my concern is that our timing is off and we wait far too long to begin serious organizational leadership training. That's why history is full of both unethical and incompetent leaders. I'd like your help to change society by thinking differently about how we raise leaders, identifying them early and developing them intentionally. That's the power of the 10-13 Window.

Chapter 8

What Every Kid Should Know

Theme: Whether a child is preconditioned to be a leader or not, she or he should understand the social process of leadership.

In Chapter 6, I offered eight indicators of children who possess a high level of leadership aptitude, and in the previous chapter, explained why we should begin accelerated leadership training between the ages of 10 and 13. But now I'd like to encourage all parents to make sure they help their child understand how leadership works. This may seem like a contradiction of what I've been advocating, namely the importance of assessing your child's leadership aptitude, so let me explain why ALL children benefit from participating in peer-led, team-oriented activities at an early age.

First of all, as we've stated before, the goal of helping children between the ages of 3 and 9 experience leadership development activities is to see who rises to the occasion. We want to offer opportunities for kids to lead projects so we can observe those who enjoy and are good at leading their peers in accomplishing goals as a team. The benefit of this is two-fold. First, we are offering young leaders an opportunity to practice skills that acknowledge their natural talents. A second benefit is to identify kids who will most likely benefit from more concentrated training, offering them a big head start. Because most children are led by adults, we often subdue kids' abilities to lead. With an intentional program that allows children to lead their peers in task-oriented team projects, we can see who will likely excel with more focused training.

A second reason every child needs to understand leadership is so they become familiar with how leadership works from various angles. Everyone is involved in leadership, either as a leader or as a participant. If you look at history, you'll realize that when the masses fail to understand how leadership works, they are vulnerable to being manipulated by unethical despots. Countless people have died because good people complied with the ideas and beliefs of evil leaders. Therefore, through team-oriented, project-based experiences facilitated by trained adults, we offer all children an opportunity to better understand what it feels like to be led by a peer. The goal is to empower children so they can avoid following those who are trying to use them to accomplish goals that hurt people. When non-leaders understand how leadership functions, how individuals obtain power, and how they get people to follow them, they can decide to follow or not follow those who are ineffective and/or unethical.

The reason is that true leadership is voluntary, meaning that leaders need others to trust them and give them power. If people decide not to follow an individual, that person ceases to be a leader. Throughout history, entire societies have rebelled against unethical leaders, resulting in their removal or even their death. At the same time, when ignorant people follow ineffective and/or unethical leaders, they will eventually regret their actions as society suffers. Therefore, everyone needs to understand how the leadership process works and how leaders obtain and use power, so that non-leaders can be empowered to make strong choices.

A third reason all young children can benefit by participating in project-based leadership training is that they learn what it means to work together as effective team members. As I've said before, one of the topics I've taught at the university level for the last 20 years is organizational leadership. There's a lot of research that focuses on how effective teams function as well as what qualities are important to being a productive team member. Think of it this way, effective team members must have two sets of skills: those required for the specific industry and those required for working well with others. These are distinct skill sets. When we focus too much on the former and too little on the latter, you wind up with really smart and talented people who disrupt the effectiveness of their teams. More organizations these days use teams, meaning that now more than ever, employees need to understand how to work with others in small, task-oriented groups. Companies today often criticize the quality of their new employees because they don't know how to work well in teams. The ability to communicate, collaborate, and manage conflict are essential skills to being valued as an employee.

As you can tell by now, I'm not a fan of suggesting that everyone can become a leader. The reason is that I have a narrower definition of the term. We'll talk more about this later. Yet I am confident that people who are not leaders possess a certain amount of power. Leaders need people to follow them, to retain and use their resources. Leaders are dealers in power. They borrow it from those who follow them for the purpose of accomplishing things together. Thus, when individuals withhold their allegiance from those who want to lead them, the power of leaders decreases and they can't produce as much. This can be good or bad, but informed and educated followers are always the key to productive organizational and social outcomes.

Our focus in KidLead is to help all children, before the age of 10, experience peer-led project-based methods. The goal at age 10 is to identify those who possess an elevated aptitude for leading and invite them into an accelerated leadership skills training program. When adults are educated on the process of leadership, they can help their children make good choices in terms of who they follow and how to function as an effective team member. The world is better when everyone understands how leadership works, along with who is and is not an effective and ethical leader.

Chapter 9

Removing Five Common Barriers

Theme: How adults stand in the way of their children's leadership development, and what to do about it.

Imagine you're at the mall with your child. You're walking past a store when one of the clerks steps out from the store, holds out her foot, and trips your child. No doubt you'd be upset. You'd probably yell something at the sinister employee, push the adult away from your child, pick up your child and go into the store to report the clerk to her manager. Naturally, as a good parent you're motivated to protect your kids and remove obstacles that could trip them.

I know this example is a bit of an exaggeration, but adults often trip up the progress of their children's leadership development. They unknowingly behave in ways that are detrimental to children learning how to lead. Well intentioned or not, we risk setting them back if we do not recognize how we're shutting them down. So before we get into proactively developing their leadership potential in future chapters, we need to address common ways that adults diminish their children's leadership development. Here are five I've observed.

The first is punishing a child for being assertive. Kids who are wired to lead sometimes exhibit behavior that is considered disrespectful and belligerent to adults. This varies from family to family and culture to culture. Some family traditions believe that children should be silent and passive around adults. Whenever a child speaks out or tries to assert himself, he gets reprimanded. "Be quiet. Go to your room. I'm the parent; you aren't." We'll talk more about ideas for effectively disciplining leaders, but punishment is somewhat different from helping a child develop self-discipline. Punishment involves threatening or inflicting some type of pain to extinguish a behavior. What you want to do is reinforce positive behaviors. So while we'll talk more about it in the future, at this point, begin becoming aware of when and for what you reprimand or punish your child, and see which of these behaviors may be symptoms of young leaders trying to express themselves, such as offering ideas, initiating action, or standing up to perceived unfairness.

A second way adults thwart leadership development is by labeling a young leader as a trouble-maker. This is more common in schools than homes, but sometimes I hear parents introducing their child as, "This is Ben; he's my out-of-control child" or "This is Sara. Don't give her a minute; she'll talk your ear off." Kids are impressionable, so when they hear a significant person in their life make less than complimentary comments about them, they'll tend to accept them as reality. But most people in this category aren't parents. They're in charge of young leaders, especially educators. Because schools value compliance and because they need to teach so many students at one time, teachers don't value noncompliance and are not trained how to effectively handle non-compliant children. They tend to try to intimidate them or send the student to the principal's office. Leaders by nature tend to be non-compliant. They feel comfortable persuading their peers and distracting them from the teacher and tasks. Some of the finest leaders have experienced conduct issues in school, primarily because schools don't understand leaders. Therefore, your job as a parent is to advocate for your child, especially if you notice that he or she has a strong aptitude for leading. If you begin hearing reports about issues related to influence, this is a sign that you may need to educate the teacher.

Suggest that she read the KidLead book or enroll your child in a different class or school. Labels tend to influence a child, so you want to make sure adults don't mistake your budding leader as a troublemaker.

A third common barrier for young leaders is being treated the same as others. We've mentioned this before, but since it fits here, I want to discuss it further. In a graduate class I teach at USC, we focus on human performance and motivation. One theory we study is justice theory. We distinguish between equity and equality. Equity means offering a sense of fairness. For example, we want to offer people with disabilities a chance to demonstrate their skills with everyone else. Equality is the idea that we're all equal, the same. Children are not the same, thus they're not equal, yet we want to treat them with equity. This requires a lot more work for adults who interact with children, because we need to understand their strengths and weaknesses.

When we pretend that young leaders are like everyone else, we avoid developing their unique gifts and abilities. So start looking for the natural strengths and abilities in your children, along with personality, in order to adjust the way you respond to them. Every great leader was at one time a child, so consider the possibility that you may be raising someone with a high aptitude for leading others.

A fourth common barrier preventing children from learning to lead is sort of the second half of the previous issue. It involves failing to offer a child who is talented in leadership the opportunities to experience accelerated training. Imagine having a child who exhibits exceptional ability in the area of academics, arts, or athletics, but the parent or educator does nothing to intentionally help that child train at a higher level. One thing well-meaning parents do is overstimulating their children with constant activities. Instead of focusing on areas that complement their strengths, they keep them continually busy with diverse classes and events. Entertainment is different from development. Busyness can be the equivalent of skimming a rock across the top of a pond. When you discover an aptitude, you want to go deeper. A big problem here is that leadership is typically considered an adult behavior, so we assume kids can't learn how to lead effectively. Another issue is that hardly any training exists in this field designed for young leaders. That's the primary mission of KidLead, focusing on assessments and project-based training curricula for the very young.

Since that's been my main focus since 2009, I'll offer you an array of ideas in this book.

And finally, a fifth common barrier that adults put in the way of their child developing leadership skills is doing too much for them. Let me say this another way. A lot of parents and teachers confuse making life easy for children with loving them. Let's face it, there's a natural desire to serve those we care for deeply, but by making things easier, we often end up limiting their growth and development. That's not love. This is one of the most difficult parenting behaviors to address because we feel like it's our job to care for and protect our children. Actually, our primary job is to set them up to succeed in life. The problem is that we do a disservice to our children when we do too much for them.

As a professor, I even see parents trying to control the lives of their young adults who are attending college, not realizing that they're undermining their confidence and self-reliance. This issue can be a problem for any child, but it's especially problematic for young leaders because they tend to possess a natural drive to accomplish things and enjoy designing plans for achievement. Natural leaders enjoy the challenge of facing a problem, figuring out potential solutions, and then taking action. So when you fail to engage your child in activities that spawn self-sufficiency, you end up creating a passive follower instead of a confident leader. Give your child room to be in charge, to initiate projects, and to let them figure out things on their own. Don't over-protect them. You're raising a future adult, not a child.

There's a story of a little girl who watched a caterpillar turn into a cocoon. Day after day, she watched the cocoon, waiting for a butterfly to emerge from it. One day, she began to see the cocoon move and gradually, the head of the butterfly peeked out of the shell. But as she watched the butterfly struggle to free itself, the girl felt sorry for it and decided to gently break open the cocoon. The new butterfly, free from its surroundings, then fell to the table with still damp, folded wings. But as the hours went by, the wings never unfolded and the butterfly never flew. The child was upset, telling her mother what happened. The wise woman comforted her daughter and then explained, "I know you meant well and were trying to help the butterfly, but the butterfly needed to struggle to get out of its cocoon. That's how young butterflies strengthen their wings so they can fly. If we make it too easy for them, they can't turn into the beautiful creatures they were created to be."

Young leaders need to be challenged. They need the freedom that allows them to take risks and accomplish tasks by leading others. Wise parents see the barriers that prevent their children from developing their leadership potential. Some of these are subtle and well-intended, but they can actually hinder a child from becoming the confident, resourceful leader who can lead others effectively.

Chapter 10

Developing KiddieLeaders (Ages 2-5)

Theme: Practical ideas for developing leadership potential among preschoolers.

Once or twice a week and if we're lucky, three times, my wife and I get photos or videos of our granddaughters. We cherish these because we live so far away from our oldest son and his family. He works for Duke University, near the East Coast, while we live near Los Angeles on the West Coast. So even though our three sons are now adults, we're reliving the days of raising preschoolers through our two granddaughters. It is such a fun and active stage, filled with questions, soaking up knowledge, and seemingly two speeds: on and off.

So while leadership training is common among adults and rare among youth, it's unheard of among preschoolers. That's what's so interesting about my work over the last several years as we've trained with and observed children as young as 3. We prototyped our first KiddieLead program with a private school in Silicon Valley, as well as working with preschool experts around the United States. Here's what we've learned about working with the very, very young in terms of leadership and leader development.

One thing we've noticed is that you can begin observing leadership behaviors among kids as young as 2. It primarily has to do with when children begin socializing and exhibiting playtime actions that other kids respond to in terms of organizing them. When you talk to preschool teachers and caregivers, they'll note that certain kids tend to emerge as the bosses of others, initiate activities, and are naturally followed by peers. This makes sense because leadership is primarily a social construct, whereby individuals help others accomplish together what they would not or could not by themselves. So the kids with a predisposition to lead tend to exhibit these behaviors in social settings very early. It may be a preschooler who announces to her classmates that they're going to play school. "I'll be the teacher and Robbie, you sit here and Kelsey, you sit over there." It can also be a boy on the playground who says, "Let's play freeze tag." Then he proceeds to give rules and directions. The others comply.

Another thing we've noticed is that typically, the younger the children, the smaller the group size. Often, a little leader will only enlist one or two peers in activities. Although a group of two people doesn't seem like much of a group, in organizational behavior, a group is defined as two or more people. The logical reason for smaller groups is that leading is not easy, so when you have very little experience in doing it, you'll tend to begin more simply. Another reason is that kids in this stage are quite self-centered and individualistic, so that getting several peers to follow them is more difficult than at older ages. This is why in our KiddieLead training curriculum we recommend teams of three to four, but in our preteen and teen programs we recommend teams of four to seven.

Sometimes, children who are the stronger leaders come across as bossy, in that they tell the other kids what to do instead of asking them politely. Naturally, they're just starting to use their talent, so they're not very good at it. We know that the best leaders are strong without being bossy. Yet many adults who aren't strong leaders or who are underdeveloped in their skills come across as bossy, too.

One more interesting thing we've noticed in young children with strong leadership capacity is that they like to be selected as the teacher's helper. At first, I disagreed with the preschool teachers when they told me this because in my experience with preteens and teens, stronger leaders don't like to be helpers; they like being in charge. But the more I observed the children, I came to agree with them. The reason, it seems, is that young children who like to lead enjoy working with the authority figure and being under the umbrella of power that the adult in charge conveys.

This and a couple other differences between ages 2 to 5 and older kids caused us to create a different assessment that estimates leadership aptitude. The Social Influence Survey is an online instrument that adults complete on children under 6. Astute teachers will strive to identify students who enjoy and are good at being in charge, and then recruit them to be the teacher's helpers. This extends the educator's authority and reduces the amount of distractions that talented leaders can create when their leadership skills are not engaged appropriately.

So before we end this chapter, let me offer a few things you can do to begin teaching leadership to preschoolers.

First, the goal in this stage is to teach all kids about working together on a team. In organizational behavior, a team is defined as a group that is focused on accomplishing a task or goal. As we mentioned, kids at this developmental phase are self-centered. Things such as sharing toys or working together on a project tend to be unnatural and difficult. Yet because most of their lives they'll be working with others, this is a great time to get them into team activities.

Another reason for doing team activities is to see who emerges as a leader. As I've mentioned, I grew up on a farm. When my dad was going to plant oats, he'd roll different types of seed in cloth and then place them in a shallow pan with water in the window with sunlight. He called these seed dolls because they looked a bit like cloth dolls. The goal was to see which seeds germinated the best. He then chose the best seeds to plant in the field so he'd get the best yield. This is like our work with preschoolers and 6- to 9-year-olds, creating a leader incubator to see who emerges, is comfortable being in charge, and who other kids follow.

Another benefit of doing team projects with a team leader is to help children learn what it's like to be peer-led. Throughout most of a child's life, adults are the leaders. We tell them what to do and when and how to do it. But when they're peer-led, children learn to problem solve on their own. This organic, experiential learning method is messier, but it's more effective.

A final reason for very young leader development is that you don't have to read or write to lead. Soft skills like leadership are primarily learned experientially, not academically. Children already enjoy games, projects, and activities, so you're merely tapping into their natural habitat by having them work together and encouraging team leaders. Keep four things in mind: First, make sure it's an activity that can be done in groups of three or four. Second, identify a team leader for the activity. Third, run the activity and then talk about leadership and working as a team. And fourth, keep it fun! Remember, this is a social project, even if you know what you're striving to accomplish. So keep it enjoyable. Adult facilitation and encouragement will make the learning far more effective, through the structure and coaching.

While organizational leadership training for preschoolers is novel and for the most part unheard of, I'm a strong advocate of it because it offers opportunities for kids to start learning how to work well in peer-led teams, along with giving children with leadership ability an opportunity to sprout. Plus it's the time in our lives when we're most pliable for character development. We start recognizing the difference between right and wrong around age 2, so if we want to develop ethical leaders, we need to think earlier rather than later.

By providing leadership training at such a young age, you'll be offering all children skill development they'll need as strong team members, and a few, sample opportunities to lead. By the age of 10, your strongest leaders will be ready for more accelerated and sophisticated training. Every great leader throughout history was at one time a 2- to 5-year-old. Imagine how effective and ethical they'd have been if they had received training like this as a preschooler.

Chapter 11

Developing Leaders (Ages 6-13)

Theme: What you should know about leadership development for years 6 through 13.

In third grade, I attended a small school in rural Iowa. I am an only child, so I loved school because when I was there, I didn't have to work on our family farm. But one thing I didn't like about third grade was my teacher. Her name was Mrs. Stuart. She was kind of mean, and she didn't appreciate my leadership because I could get my fellow students to ignore her and focus on something else. I didn't understand it at the time, but I was a class leader. Because Mrs. Stuart didn't like my influence, she gave me a low grade in conduct, which got me in trouble with my parents.

You don't want to be a Mrs. Stuart in the life of a child. I'm sure that Mrs. Stuart would be sad if she knew that I considered her a negative person in my life, even as an adult. Sometimes parents, educators, and people who work with children can influence them negatively without even knowing it. In this chapter, we'll discuss leadership development among elementary school children ages 6 to 12. Let's divide this stage into two parts: ages 6 to 9 (early childhood) and years 10 to 12 (preteens).

As I explained in a previous chapter, we've learned that at age 10, a child with exceptional leadership talent is ready for more accelerated training. But prior to that, children are still in early developmental stages of their social-emotional and cognitive development. Therefore, we recommend continuing the type of leadership development training that we explained in the chapter on preschoolers, ages 2 to 5. The difference is that by age 6, most children are a bit more familiar with working in groups and socializing with their peers, so you may want to consider increasing the size of teams to three to five members. Again, the smaller the team size, typically the easier it is to organize it. The larger the size, the more challenging it is.

The primary goals in early childhood are helping students experience peer-led projects, along with identifying those with exceptional leadership gifts. Children with strong talent are often perceived to be strong-willed and bossy. The best place to look for these natural abilities is during playtime, when adults are not directly supervising. The reason is that adults tend to alter social behavior, either by taking the role of an authority figure or intimidating child leaders with their presence. Look for children who gain the respect of their peers, initiating actions such as a recess activity, or who seem to take charge in projects. You can use the NYLI assessment instrument to estimate leadership aptitude. An adult who has observed a child in social settings completes the online survey on a student. Once you begin identifying students who demonstrate a natural aptitude for leading, you will want to offer them more opportunities to lead formally, such as putting them in charge of team projects, asking them to be in charge if you need to step away, or suggesting formal roles such as class representative, club president, or the like.

By the age of 10, students demonstrating a gift for leading should be recruited into intentional programs to develop their potential. This is the age to offer accelerated project-based training such as LeadNow. In the United States, this is typically Grades 4 through 6. A growing trend is for elementary schools to run through fifth grade and then middle schools to include Grades 6 through 8.

We've discovered that eighth graders typically behave more like adults than sixth and seventh graders, so again, it's why we discuss the 10-13 Window. But while individual development is more specific, sometimes it's best to keep students in groups where they socialize, as in schools.

By the age of 10, students with leadership aptitude possess the ability to think more critically and can begin learning more sophisticated social skills required for leading. These include persuasion, motivation, communication, and problem solving, as well as recognizing abilities in others. This combination is important for leaders of all ages; therefore, it's foundational for teaching preteens how to lead.

One question we're asked a lot is, "How do you avoid creating an elitist attitude among children identified to participate in accelerated programs such as Kidlead?" We've found that the attitude begins with adults. Elitism conveys the attitude that I'm better than you, that gifted children are more valuable than normal kids. But obviously this is not true, because all kids possess equal value and should be respected. Yet, *better than* is not the same as *different than*. Students with exceptional abilities are different than others. Therefore, whether it is academic ability, athletic potential, or artistic talent, kids with exceptional potential should be offered opportunities to help them reach their full potential. We want to start leadership training at a young age so we can teach them humility and service, and to honor all people regardless of their talent or ability.

So if you pull out certain children for specialized leadership training, what do you do with the other children? In a perfect world, we would be able to recognize strengths in all children so that we could invite everyone into developmental programs that match their talents. But unfortunately, society doesn't do this well. Instead, we keep everyone together and rarely offer accelerated training for those identified with exceptional talent. If you have children in leadership training who do not seem to be good at leading or if you want to take an entire class through some sort of leadership training, we recommend giving the opportunities to lead to the students gifted in leadership. The rest can continue to learn how to be strong team members in peer-led teams.

Preteens are typically considered as ages 8 to 12. But in our years of work with thousands of children and youth, we've found that there's a significant jump in social-emotional maturity between ages 9 and 10. So while you may see some kids ready for more complex project-based training at 9, you'll run into problems if you allow some but not all 9-year-olds into a program. Thus, 10 seems to be a good starting age for both boys and girls who possess a high aptitude for leading. Because children at this stage are still concrete thinkers, meaning they take things literally and are not yet conceptual thinkers, project-based, experiential learning is the best. This is often referred to as learn-by-doing. Merely reading or talking about leadership isn't likely to do much to improve skills. Plus you'll likely bore children, creating a negative perception of leadership and thus causing them to avoid it.

Someone once said, "The shoe should never tell the foot how big it can grow." Effective parents and educators look at the child and then strive to create opportunities that match the aptitude they observe. By doing this, we set up our children to succeed and offer them a significant head start in acquiring skills that will serve them and society throughout their lives. Elementary ages are critical for giving all students opportunities to experience teams and then transitioning those with observable leadership giftedness into accelerated training. Every great leader was at one time a 6- to 13-year-old. Why not identify them early, to create a successful trajectory for their lives?

Chapter 12

Developing Adolescent Leaders

Theme: What you should know about leadership development for teens.

Years ago, when I was in graduate school, I was among the first who purchased Apple's McIntosh computer. Even though I am a relatively intelligent adult and the Mac was an improvement from early DOS computers, I still had a learning curve because I lacked experience. Now, even though I'm not strong in IT or computers, it's not as big of a deal when I break in a new computer because I have many years of experience.

Here's my point. Teens, ages 14 years and up, should be considered adults who merely lack life experience. For all practical purposes, they possess the capacity to learn and lead like many adult leaders, but they've never had opportunities to be trained or practice these skills. Few if any of them have led formally, and most won't be given official opportunities to lead until adulthood. Yet, physically and intellectually, they're far more like us than their younger predecessors. We'll talk more about puberty in the next chapter, but let's focus specifically on leadership development differences for 14- to 18-year-olds.

There are four primary things to consider when preparing leadership development training for teenagers.

First, leadership giftedness is important, but not essential. All along, we've been talking about the importance of identifying a high aptitude for leading that we refer to as The O Factor, which basically means a natural talent and gift for organizational leading. Like athleticism, art, and academics, giftedness is defined as the top 3% to 5%, those wired to excel in certain areas. We expand this range in our program to 10% and sometimes 20% to avoiding missing sleeper leaders who may have been discouraged by parents or educators or cultural norms. Realistically, less than 10% are predispositioned to lead, regardless of their age. But as a person matures, life experience can at times translate into levels of leadership ability. That's why the younger you begin, the more important it is to focus on giftedness, since life experience is so low.

The challenge we've noted for children under 10 is that because leadership is a sophisticated social skill, you need a certain level of cognitive and social-emotional maturity to effectively train them. Thus, during ages 10-13, giftedness is essential. But during years 14-18, students have gained more life experience in groups and organizations. So while giftedness is still important, it's not as essential as in the preteen stage. You'll want to do an NYLI assessment on potential participants so that you can keep a critical mass of students with high leadership aptitude in your training group, but more emotionally mature students can still participate as team members and in leading less difficult projects.

A second consideration for adolescent leadership development training is to continue focusing on project-based methods. The reason this continues to be a key approach to leader skill cultivation is that soft skills such as leading are primarily gained through active, experiential learning. As we've stated before, leadership is a social skill that is difficult to gain through lectures, reading, or more academic and cerebral processes. You'll want to make sure that whatever curriculum you use or design involves letting students actually lead their peers in task-oriented processes. By this age, they're ready for more complicated projects, so we add layers of complexity that increase the difficulty.

Our LeadWell curriculum is modeled after many executive training programs that incorporate mini-projects, completed in 15-30 minutes, along with real-time coaching and then a debrief at the end. This type of training allows students to experience peer-led projects that allow both the Team Leaders to lead as well as team members to learn how to be productive participants.

A third and strategic developmental change between preteens and teens is that teens are conceptual thinkers. This tends to happen a bit sooner for girls than boys, but by 14, most young men and women are able to think beyond black and white. So while we continue to use project-based methods for skill development, we can expand the debrief discussions to include concepts such as leadership, influence, power, vision, strategy, and conflict management. That's why in our LeadWell training curriculum, we include a book and assign short readings that explain the underlying principle we're learning in the activities. This ties concepts with tactics. Leadership, power, and influence are complex social dynamics, but when you're in a room with teens possessing strong leadership aptitude, you're amazed at how well they process these issues, along with expressing their own strengths and weaknesses. Those of us who interact with young leaders stay motivated by the keen insights they gain and the self-revealing insights they share.

A fourth element in this developmental stage is offering them a dose of real-world leadership experience. Most of our project-based methods are accomplished somewhat quickly in a classroom or open space setting. They typically complete the activity in 20-40 minutes. But because teens are pretty much young adults in their capacity to think and perform in social settings, merely lacking experience, we find it important to provide a structure to design and implement a project that they activate publicly. That's why half of the LeadWell training curriculum involves a strategic planning model that gives them a somewhat guided yet flexible process for creating, planning, implementing, and debriefing a project.

This could be something like helping their school become more ecology-minded, raising money for a charity, recruiting a group of students to clean up a local playground, or even running a school assembly to promote a new program. This involves dividing the project into steps and letting students take turns running 10-minute meetings. Because leaders must facilitate meetings all their lives, this provides opportunities to practice and become familiar with a strategic meeting process. What's even more amazing is that their peers are taught how to provide constructive feedback to help the Team Leader know what she did well and how she could be even better next time. Because it is future-oriented, we called it feed-forward, not feed-back. At the end of the project, the teens do a post-mortem on the project to discuss what they learned, how they could do better next time, and of course to celebrate the victory. Leaders need to know how to applaud the team for hard work.

The first 20 years of life are truly a miracle. We come into the world as helpless infants, dependent on others to feed, bathe, nurture, and protect us. Yet before our second decade of life, some of us possess the ability to lead groups of people in accomplishing together what they would not or could not as individuals. There is no reason to wait until a person turns 30, 40, or 50 to train them to lead organizationally. While character pliability slows considerably during the teen years, cognitive and social-emotional development open unique and exciting possibilities. Society underestimates teenagers' ability to learn and demonstrate complex social behaviors like leading. We'll talk more about that in our next chapter as we focus on puberty.

Chapter 13

The GPS for Navigating Puberty

Theme: Assisting young leaders as they transition to adulthood.

As I've mentioned before, I was raised with the strong impression that there was room for only one leader in my family, and it wasn't me. As you can imagine, there were some tense times between my father and me, especially during my teen years. One of the most dynamic events took place when I was 16. My dad wanted me to keep my hair short, so one Saturday morning he told me to get a haircut. I drove to the barber and got it cut. My hair felt short to me. During lunch, my father said, "I thought I told you to get a haircut." "I did," I responded, pointing to my head. "You didn't get it cut short enough. You need to go back and tell them to cut more off." <u>I was mad</u>. I went back to the barber and had them cut off more. I felt embarrassed to have such short hair, especially during a time when long hair among teens was popular. By the time my second haircut was finished, I was so angry at my dad that I decided to run away. I went over to a friend's house. He was older than me and probably much wiser. He eventually convinced me that it wouldn't be smart to run away and that I'd eventually need to go home. Even though it was late, I took my friend's advice.

While every family is different, that story exemplifies what many parents and teens experience. Although this chapter is applicable to parenting in general, before we're through you'll see why it's so important among children wired to lead.

A few years ago, I read a book called *Teen 2.0*. The author is Dr. Robert Epstein, a research psychologist. I was so impressed with the book and how it relates to raising leaders that I contacted him. When I discovered that he lives in the San Diego, California area, I offered to take him to lunch so we could have a deeper conversation. Dr. Epstein's research focused on why teen years are so commonly known for their rebelliousness. When he began looking at this stage historically, he discovered that it's a relatively modern phenomenon. In Western society, you don't see significant issues of youth rebelliousness until the late 1800s. As he looked deeper, he realized that adolescence is a modern social construct. Rebelliousness emerged as a youth issue when they began living at home longer. This trend increases with the start of the Information Age, as children stay in school longer to prepare for life in a more complex society.

Historically, people began transitioning to adulthood much younger than we currently think. Epstein notes a variety of cultural ceremonies and events that take place between years 12-14, marking the transition to adulthood. These include events such as catechism, the Bar Mitzva, and the aboriginal walk-about. Until the last 200 years, people were apprenticing for their professions by the age of 14, seeking a mate, and starting a family. Physically and cognitively, humans reflect adulthood by the ages of 13 and 14. Until public education became the norm, teens pretty much entered the adult world. As the need to stay in school lengthened, we kept teens with their own ages, slowing the social maturation process. Yet teens for the most part feel significantly different from their preteen counterparts.

The problem, Epstein notes, is infantilizing, meaning we treat these young adults as infants and children and they naturally rebel against this. Imagine if your boss lectured you and did not treat you as an adult. Hopefully your supervisor doesn't, and I'm assuming that if you're a boss you don't treat your staff that way. Regardless, no adult wants to feel disrespected and treated like a child.

Therefore, when parents fail to shift gears in how they think of, communicate with, and respond to their adolescent sons and daughters, they're going to create unnecessary conflict. Some parents may say, "But my children aren't rebelling. They're quite compliant." That may be true, but either they're masking their frustration out of respect for or fear of you or they're legitimately letting you run their lives. Either way, you may be setting back your offspring and reducing their confidence.

Here are three things to consider when you're parenting a child around the age of 12. This may be a year earlier if your child is a female or a year older if your child is a male, and obviously, each child is different, but be careful not to let your parental projections of "your little baby" hinder your approach during adolescence.

First, have "the talk." In our culture, "the talk" usually means sex education. Obviously, that's important. But by "the talk," I'm referring to a heart-to-heart conversation to let your child know that you know she is getting older and that you'll begin treating her more like an adult. That means you'll be raising the expectations of responsibility, but with it will come greater freedom. It will progress over the next few years but will start soon. Depending on your culture or family traditions, you may even want to design a ceremony to create a memorable milestone. These vary, but recognizing this transition formally marks a new chapter for her and your relationship with her.

Second, begin introducing opportunities for you to follow up on this discussion. You and your spouse will want to discuss options, whether this involves changing chores and family expectations, TV viewing, bedtimes, or any number of other situations in family life and parenting. When this happens, spell out the decision options and consequence differences. Provide feedback, not in a condescending, parental attitude, but rather in a mentor-protégé mode. For many parents, it may help if you think of it more like a professional and business context, where you're developing adults in subordinate roles. Obviously you still love your child, but everyone is intentionally transitioning toward an adult-parenting relationship.

Here's an example: "Jenny, your father and I are going out to dinner on Friday night. We may not be back until late. Although we usually get someone to come in and watch you and your brother, we think you're now old enough to take care of yourself and your brother. We trust your decisions and will support you if your brother doesn't cooperate. Do you feel comfortable doing this?"

And finally, a third thing you can do is increase the amount of responsibilities and freedoms as the child develops. One of the topics I teach at USC graduate school is on performance and motivation. Little discourages and demotivates a human more than not being acknowledged and rewarded for progress. Naturally, giving a young person responsibility also runs the risk of failure, disappointment, and discouragement. But most adults realize that they're greatest life lessons came via their failures more than their successes. Figure out what motivates your adolescent and then reward behaviors you desire.

One thing Dr. Epstein said that stuck with me is that adolescents aren't seeking freedom as much as they are longing for responsibility. That's the big difference between true adulthood and childhood. While your teen may be expressing a desire for more freedom, the greatest honor for them is to be given responsibility. That brings me back to the premise of this book. Our primary focus in KidLead is helping adults develop the leadership potential in their children. Leaders are responsible for the organizations they serve and the people on their teams. By helping young leaders experience responsibility in a safe and loving environment, we set them up to succeed. Although this approach to parenting is good for all children and will enhance your relationship with your child, the bigger picture is how it can develop young leaders to be responsible for the goals of the organization and the needs of the people they lead.

Chapter 14

Turning Home into a Leader Incubator

Theme: Five ideas for leveraging family life to develop your child's leadership potential.

When our middle son was a senior in college, he was invited to interview with JP Morgan investment bank in San Francisco. My wife and I were flying from California to Florida to do training for KidLead, so it just happened that we would be crossing paths in the San Francisco airport. Nancy and I saw Josh as he walked down the hall toward us, in his business suit, carrying his leather computer bag. It was one of those moments when you look at your spouse and say, "Our little boy is all grown up."

We greeted each other and then I asked, "Josh, did you ever think you'd be interviewing for a job at JP Morgan?"

He said, "Dad, I've been imagining this my whole life."

As I thought about it, he was right. He'd been seeing himself in roles like this for much of his life.

When you're raising a child or youth with strong leadership ability, you'll be interacting with a child who is highly self-motivated and has a sense of destiny. Therefore, it's important for you to create a home life that supports your child's future dreams and aspirations. Here are five practical ideas for creating a family culture where young leaders can thrive.

Firstly, begin with the end in mind. Imagine your child as an accomplished, self-actualized adult. Wise parents understand they don't own their children, but rather they've been entrusted with an opportunity to influence them for a few fleeting years. What is the legacy you want to leave with your children? How do you want them to remember you? Visualize them as healthy, vibrant, productive adults and then build a path to assist them in becoming this type of person. We tell adults that developing young leaders begins between your ears, meaning they need to start thinking differently about their children. As we do this, we begin treating them differently and as we've noted before, people strive to become as they're treated.

Second, think of leadership development as a ramp. You want to gradually increase responsibilities and rewards as you see your young leader progress. The goal is to offer more and larger opportunities to challenge them. Naturally this needs to be demonstrated and progressive. You can't dump a big task on a 10-year-old until they've proven themselves in medium-sized tasks. This shouldn't come until they've succeeded in smaller projects. One of the strongest human motivators is what we call stretch goals. These are periodic challenges that stretch a person to achieve more than they have in the past. Begin small, but work up the ramp.

Third, utilize home projects. These possess the same ingredients for any leadership project, but you'll use everyday home and family situations to develop your child's leadership potential. The three ingredients are a goal, a team, and a risk.

    1. A goal has to do with what you want to have accomplished.

The key is to focus on the "what" instead of the "how." Parents often prevent their children from developing problem-solving skills by telling them exactly how to accomplish a task, but leaders especially enjoy the challenge of figuring things out their way. One leadership theory is called Path-Goal. Researchers observe how leaders select different paths from each other to remove barriers and accomplish goals. Rarely do they do it the same way.

2. The second ingredient is a team. This is essential to leadership development, because leaders help people accomplish together what they would not or could not by themselves. Individuals can do chores, but leaders accomplish tasks with and through others. Therefore, you'll need to figure out who is available to become team members (or let your child figure that out). This could be you and your spouse, siblings, other family members, and friends. We recommend at least two others because it's a completely different dynamic to influence one person.

3. The third ingredient is a risk. By risk we mean the child must have authority to be in charge and the ability to make a decision, whether good or bad. Another risk is that resources should be involved, whether it's money, time, or other things. If there's no risk involved, then it's probably not about leading. Leaders must become familiar with handling pressure. Naturally, the risk should begin small and then increase, like the ramp we mentioned. There should be the opportunity to fail, otherwise it's unlike life. This also creates more pressure for parents, because we don't like to clean up messes and we inherently want to reduce risk for our children, but in doing so, we hinder their development.

Here's an example of a leadership home project. Ask your 12-year-old to be a Meal Manager. Traditionally a parent might ask a child to prepare dinner, but managing a meal is quite different. You might say, "Honey, your dad and I have to attend a meeting next Thursday. We won't be home until 7pm, so you're the Meal Manager. You need to use a team. You have us and your brother, or you can recruit a couple of your friends. You decide what we're going to eat, when we're going to eat, and who is going to get the food, prepare it, and then clean up. We'll give you a budget to spend, but you can't go over it. You'll also need to work with our schedules, since we won't be home until 7pm and your brother has basketball practice after school. As the Meal Manager, it's your job to create a plan and make sure that your team members know their roles and stay within the budget."

While seemingly simple, this has many of the same dynamics that every leadership project has: an objective, a need for a plan, limited resources, team members, talent, and potential conflict. After the meal, make sure you have a time to debrief, seeing what your child learned and how he or she might go about it differently next time. If it turns out well, great. If it doesn't turn out well, great. Building a leader is more important than making a meal. Be careful not to give a lot of advice, and if you do, ask permission first. This helps your 12-year-old feel like the boss.

A fourth idea for developing your child's leadership potential is to leverage media. There are many movies, television shows, story books, and even some video games that include situations where a leader influences others to follow. Sometimes this is for good and sometimes for bad, but all of these become opportunities to discuss leadership. For example, if you're watching a Disney show where a preteen is getting his friends together to help another friend, you can pause the program during an interesting scene and talk about the various characters, helping your child identify who the leader is, and then discussing whether you think the leader is being effective or not. Or on the ride home from a movie, you can talk about the various characters and identify which ones were leaders and what they did.

A fifth idea for developing your child's leadership potential is to make it fun. Kids and teens like having fun. If we make leadership projects overly stressful or negative, they'll grow up resenting being a leader and avoid learning how to lead. Make sure you don't make failures a big deal, because you want them to grow through it, not just go through it. You're offering what few leaders ever get in life: an environment to learn how to lead that is forgiving and accepting. By making this process enjoyable, you're also creating a happy home and making memories for years to come.

Chapter 15

Advocating for Your Young Leader

Theme: Five ideas for leveraging family life to develop your child's leadership potential.

We've been talking about how to identify and develop your child's leadership potential because we need to start leadership development while leaders are pliable. By doing this, we set up our children for success (especially if they possess natural leadership talent). Plus, society needs more effective and ethical leaders than ever before.

Although you may be interested in developing your child's leadership potential, you can't presume that others share your interest. Throughout history, people have perceived that leading is for adults, not kids. Therefore, you're going against centuries of tradition by striving to help your child learn to lead so young. So while you'll want to create a home life that allows your child to lead, you'll also need to become an advocate for child leadership, beyond your immediate family.

When I began KidLead several years ago, I assumed that since people valued leadership and loved children, they'd automatically want to develop leaders while they're still kids and youth. But after a decade of running into social norms that didn't see things my way, I realized that I needed to do a lot more education before I focused on persuasion. That's why I've written so many books and articles, and presented so many workshops and seminars, to help people understand what I've discovered. If you want people around you and your child to fan the flames of their leadership potential, no doubt you'll need to help them understand what it is you're striving to accomplish.

Naturally, you'll want to do this in a positive and constructive way instead of shaming or criticizing others, but you can't expect people to automatically share your leadership vision for your child. You don't want to come across as a Tiger Mom or convey the idea that your child is a Prima Donna or genius, but let me give you a few ideas of what you can do to help educators, caregivers, and extended family members reinforce what you're doing in your home.

#1. Tell stories. One of the best ways to educate and intrigue people with new ways of parenting and developing young leaders is to offer stories that describe your child in leadership roles. Whether this is an informal conversation with friends, social media, or a family reunion, people enjoy stories. Leaders use storytelling as a powerful tool to convey values, vision, and goals. You can simply describe a project that your child led, along with some funny outcomes or cute things your child said in the process. People listen to stories in general, but when you focus on leadership stories, you'll be able to help them catch a vision that children and youth can lead. At the same time, avoid the "my child is a genius" attitude. No one appreciates that.

#2. Explain in the moment. Sometimes you'll find yourself in a situation where people don't understand why you're doing what you're doing. For example, let's just say that you have friends over for dinner and you ask your 10-year-old to get the other children together to set the table for the meal. You may offer a couple of coaching suggestions and clarify that it's to be a team project. Your friends, overhearing your conversation, may look at you with interest. You can briefly explain how you're striving to teach your child leadership skills and this is an example of what you do on a regular basis in your family. Explain how individual chores are different from leading teams.

#3. Recommend resources. Obviously, you're a motivated parent in that you're reading a book like this. This idea fits well with the previous two. Recommend this book and The O Factor. Parents can find an array of articles on the KidLead website, along with free assessments (SIS, NYLI). While this may be a challenge if you don't know a lot of resources, make sure you have at least two or three that support what you're striving to accomplish with your children. This will give you info to share with those who ask or who need to be educated in this area.

#4. Model for others. Whenever you're in social settings with your children, people are observing you. This provides an opportunity to succeed and fail. Realize that others are watching you, so make sure you communicate your values effectively. Let your child lead. Coach them. Provide support and affirmation in such a way that others will notice that you're striving to parent differently. Sometimes they'll observe silently, without saying anything. At other times, they may compliment you or ask you to explain what you do. No doubt they'll talk about your parenting style on their way home.

#5. Insert yourself. Sometimes, when you are in a situation where another authority figure is going against what you're striving to accomplish with your child, you'll feel the need to stand up for your child. This is your opportunity and responsibility to intervene, to insert yourself into the situation and advocate for your child. Don't do this immediately, but rather observe how the teacher, coach, caregiver, or

adult is treating your child. When you realize the authority-figure is working against what you're striving to teach your child, don't just sit passively. Step in and say something, do something. Just don't go crazy, because some parents fail as good examples when this happens. When a parent stands up to authority figures who fail to recognize a child's leadership potential, that child remember those times, increasing self-confidence.

#6. Intervene as needed. There may come a time when you need to ask for your child to be placed in another class or on another team. This may be the most difficult item to implement, but because your child is your priority, it's your responsibility to be his or her primary advocate. It may mean uninviting friends who discourage your child's development in this area or not inviting neighbor's friends who deter your child from leading. Obviously, no one appreciates a parent who believes that his or her child is the best at everything. Yet as a parent, you're the most responsible for determining who is going to have access to developing your child. Naturally, this runs against the social norms of letting others influence your child according to how they think, but it elevates your role as the most important single influence. You may need to change the people who have direct contact with your child or move your child to an environment where people with the right attitude and skills can influence them.

No matter what you do, you'll need to advocate for your children if you want to maximize their leadership potential, because most adults do not understand the value of this process and are unfamiliar with how to accomplish this goal. As you do this, you'll be training the way society thinks about and develops their leaders.

Chapter 16

Aligning Your Leadership Styles

Theme: Adjusting your leadership style to fit your child's wiring.

Each of our three sons is different, even though they're from the same gene pool. Although everyone on earth is unique, there exist basic categories of personality types that impact the way we behave socially. In organizational behavior, we discuss the impact of temperament, motivation, conflict management, and leadership styles, all of which are somewhat connected to each other. While I'm not assuming that you or your child are wired to lead naturally, for the sake of this chapter, I'm going to presume that you and your child fit within one of four overarching leadership styles. The goal is to help you identify which you relate to the most, as well as your child, so that you can better understand how to align your style with your child's. This will reduce conflict and increase the development of your child's leadership potential.

Let me define four leadership styles and then offer advice on how to develop children with the same and different styles. Although each of these reflects one of four basic temperament types, our focus now is on leading. People with any of the four types can lead. For example, if you analyze the leadership styles of U.S. Presidents, you'll see all four represented. There is no one way to lead. Naturally, a leader's personality will significantly influence how he or she leads, but there is not one personality type that all leaders share. Therefore, try to avoid thinking of leaders in this way. Even though many share common qualities, they are distinct.

The first leadership style is Director. People with strengths in this style tend to reflect what many stereotypically think of as a leader. She is outgoing, strong-willed, and ready to offer her opinion, along with a suggestion to follow her. The Director feels comfortable being in charge and will often be the loudest person in a meeting or brainstorming session. Although this style is obviously strong in situations where clarity and direction are needed, the same person is less effective when sensitivity, analysis of details, and empathy are required.

The second style is Analyzer. This person can be very task-oriented and thinks deeply about problems, solutions, and strategies. The Analyzer needs time to think, ponder, and matriculate issues that impact a problem and potential solutions. Sometimes, Analyzers can appear to be quiet, aloof, and even negative, but their ability to look deeply into a project or situation makes them valuable. The downside of Analyzers is that they can be slow to decide, come across as reserved or negative, and slow the process that may require speed to succeed.

The third style is Motivator. This individual has strong people and communication skills. He makes others feel good about being involved in a project. He is enjoyable to be around because he makes us feel good about ourselves. Yet Motivators can also prove to be flighty and undependable, as they get bored quickly and feel distant from their opposites who are detail-oriented and prone to pessimism. Motivators are cheerleaders who inspire us, yet they also run the risk of seeming shallow and oblivious to details.

The fourth style is Plodder. This individual sometimes gets overlooked as a leader, yet the strength of a Plodder is that she responds well under pressure and is likeable. The Plodder has few enemies. Since leadership is a social skill, the ability to be well-liked and avoid alienating people is a strength. The weakness of a Plodder is not moving fast enough for some people and thus runs the risk of losing highly motivated people, plus a reticence to make decisions that may turn off people. Plodders might avoid confrontation and conflict that are sometimes required in leadership situations. So while Plodders are not the natural leader pick, they often possess an ability to gain followers that non-Plodders overlook.

Based on these simple definitions, how would you describe your leadership style, your spouse's, and your children's?

If you're a *Director*, you'll relate to child Directors, but you'll also run the risk of conflict because you're so similar. Butting heads refers to the conflict that arises from strong, differing opinions. Be careful not to intimidate your little Director, because as an adult, you'll likely have more power and authority. If you're a Director, you can help Analyzers and Motivators use their abilities in leading by assisting them in the areas of their weaknesses. You'll be the opposite of a Plodder, so be careful not to get irritated by his or her pace or the child's speed of decision making or level of risk taking. Encourage the child to be stronger with others.

If you're a *Motivator*, use your strengths to inspire your children. Bring out their best through encouragement and affirmation. You're well positioned as a parent to see the potential in your kids. Be careful not to over-promise and fail to follow through. Children feel disappointed when they hope for something that parents don't follow through on. Plus, don't think that your child's less-than-happy disposition is a recipe for failure. Support your child regardless of his or her temperament, but try not to overwhelm them with your positive enthusiasm.

If you're an *Analyzer*, you'll relate best to your Analyzer children. Help them develop the strengths of their style and avoid the weaknesses. Encourage them to focus on the positive and be solution-oriented. Many Analyzers are risk-averse, meaning they don't like to take chances, so you can help them by taking reasonable risks and then celebrating these, whether or not they succeed. As an Analyzer, you're the opposite of Motivators, so you'll want to pick up the pace and intentionally be more energetic when interacting with them. You'll want to have patience with Directors, because they'll want to make decisions while you're still weighing the issues.

If you're a *Plodder*, you'll relate well with your Plodder children. Yet, make sure you don't let Plodder kids be lazy, avoid conflict, or be overrun by Motivator and Director kids. You need to advocate for your Plodder leader, providing emotional space for the child to make decisions and lead. Intentionally think of ways where they can be in charge and oversee family activities. Push yourself to delegate authority and provide freedom for your more assertive children. Your strengths of support and encouragement will be appreciated, since you're naturally relational.

In summary, your ability to match leader styles with your child will go a long way in helping your young leader be comfortable in his or her style. Obviously, parents will want to work together in using their styles to influence their children effectively. If you're different from each other, this offers additional options for relating to and strengthening children. Offering two leader developers for your children will enhance the chances of them learning from you and developing their leadership potential. Understanding and matching styles is a powerful tool when used properly in families.

Chapter 17

Leveraging Your Strengths to Equip

Theme: How to maximize your resources to tap your child's potential.

When our sons were young, we lived in Scottsdale, Arizona for 10 years. Scottsdale is a beautiful city in the desert, northeast of Phoenix. During our time there, we had the boys involved in a variety of sports. We played catch in the front yard of our home, and we had a swimming pool in the backyard, along with a trampoline. They played tennis at a park near our home and baseball and basketball at the local Boys & Girls club. We rode our bikes through the neighborhoods and went on hikes in the mountains surrounding the city. During the summer, when it was hot, we went on inner tube rides down a nearby river. We took advantage of the resources we had available to develop our sons athletically.

As a dedicated parent, you're no different. You want to provide what you can for your child, from food and security, to warmth and shelter, to the best education, exercise, and technology you can afford. But what parents often overlook, especially those with kids who possess superior leadership potential, is how they can leverage their resources to develop their child's influence skills.

In another chapter, we talked about matching your leadership level with your child's, whether your child has more, less, or similar talent as you. But in this chapter I'd like to offer some ideas for leveraging other resources you may have at your disposal to help your child learn to lead. In organizational behavior we teach a concept called power resources, referring to how people influence others in an organization. A lot of people think that if you're not the boss, you have no power, but that's not true. There are multiple ways to gain influence. The same is true in raising a young leader, whether or not you're gifted at leading yourself. Here are seven ideas to help you leverage resources you may have, to develop your child's leadership ability.

First, take stock of your leadership experiences. Chances are, even if you're not gifted in leadership, you've experienced situations where leadership took place. Consider work situations where you or someone else had to lead a team of people to accomplish a task together. This is a wonderful opportunity for you to tell stories about how leadership happens. Children like stories, as long as you make them interesting and simple. Base the depth on the age of the child. Naturally, the younger the child, the more you need to simplify it. Feel free to share the challenges and failures, not just the successes.

Second, consider who you can introduce to your child. You probably have people in your network who are leaders. This is a great opportunity for your child to meet people who influence others, through your relationships. Perhaps you can take your child to a work social or have your boss over for dinner. Make the introductions. Most leaders are honored to be introduced to a child. The good ones will get down on the child's level and engage them with honor.

Third, accompany your child to decision-making groups. There are a number of meetings where you can introduce your child to the process of adults resolving problems together. This may be a homeowners' association, a school Parent Teacher Association meeting, or even a city council meeting. You may need to ask permission to attend, but many groups allow observers to view their meetings and even participate. Bring your child and then talk about the decisions that were made and what other adults did to promote or thwart the process, and ask your child for ideas to improve things.

Fourth, introduce your child to leadership books, seminars, and media. We talked about this briefly, but a good way to give your child a sense of what leaders do is to encourage reading biographies of leaders. Most libraries offer books written for various age levels on the lives of leaders in your culture. You can read these together or offer incentives to motivate your child to read these books. Ask for feedback and even a report, so there is a sense of accountability. If you're going to attend a seminar on leading, see if you can invite your child. Don't underestimate how much your child can learn, even if she or he is coloring or doodling during the process. The power of introducing your child to a leadership development course can be significant.

Fifth, recruit opportunities for your child at school and civic groups. Consider talking to adults who oversee programs where your child is involved. This could mean school, athletic teams, and other after-school and social settings. Ask if there are opportunities where your child can participate in leadership. Think about ways you could suggest involvement in more managerial tasks. Obviously you may have to get creative and brainstorm, but don't just treat your child like every other. The great thing about this idea is that if an adult is truly a leader, he or she will likely appreciate your interest and go out of their way to help your child participate in more behind-the-scenes matters. We'll talk about this more in another chapter.

Sixth, take your child to work. In the United States, there's a designated day every year where employees are encouraged to bring their children to work. This is an opportunity for a child to experience what his or her parent does, along with seeing the office, building, and colleagues. Some companies welcome this more than once a year. Obviously, you'll need to figure out if this fits your employment or not, but the idea lends itself to adults introducing their children to employment and organizational life. I'd encourage you to suggest the idea, along with customized ways for your child to see how decisions are made where you work.

Seventh, discuss work situations and ask your child's advice. Intentionally bring up work situations during dinner, weekends, or at bedtimes. Share your decisions as a boss or where you need your boss's approval or involvement. Make these age-appropriate, but let your child into your world of decision making and critical thinking, along with hearing how leadership works and organizations function. For example, let's say that someone on your team is not doing their job and it's frustrating the rest of the members. Talk about this to your child. Ask him or her for advice. "Honey, what do you think I should do?" "What do you think my boss should do?" "Should I talk to my boss about it or should I talk to the person who isn't doing her work?" "Should I ask the team to work together to talk to her?" By introducing your child to real world examples of leaders, power, influence, and problem solving, you're giving him a head start.

Consider how you can tap into your everyday resources to help your child expand his or her leadership potential. Chances are you have far more opportunities than you're using.

Chapter 18

Raising Self-Disciplined Kids

Theme: Learning to delay gratification is essential for those being prepared to lead.

The week before I began writing this chapter, the CEO of a major movie and entertainment company in the United States resigned because of an affair he had with a young actress. While the issue had moral implications, he did not do anything illegal. He was being forced out because of his indiscretion and the critical situation it created for the holding company, as it was about to put him in charge of an even larger portion of their entertainment sector. A staff member of this company was a guest lecturer in my class at USC that week. She was dumbfounded that the man, respected for his ability to lead, could not see the negative optics of the situation, where a person of power has an affair with a person without power who could benefit professionally from the relationship.

This is an adult example of how a leader's inability to be self-disciplined can impact an entire organization. History is filled with examples of these kinds of behaviors. So in this chapter, we're going to talk about ways that you can help your child develop self-discipline. Although this is beneficial to all children, it's vital for those who are preparing to lead. The reason is that leaders are dealers in power. A powerless leader is an oxymoron. The problem with power is that it tends to bring out the worst in people when they lack self-discipline. People are tempted to use their power to benefit themselves instead of others. They are susceptible to making bad choices. Because a leader's decisions impact so many others, children raised to be effective leaders need to develop self-discipline as early as possible. Here are four practices to implement.

The first practice is to reward desired behavior. It's the powerful principle of reinforcement. When I wrote *KidLead: Growing Great Leaders*, I interviewed several national leaders, asking them how they raised their children or how they were raised as children. When I asked John Maxwell what his father did to help him grow as a leader, he said, "Leaders are readers, they're always growing. One thing my dad did was pay me to read books of great leaders. It's interesting that a lot of parents pay their children to do home chores like take out the trash. That's fine if you want to raise a trash collector." So one thing to consider when raising a self-disciplined child is to establish rewards for behaviors that reflect qualities you want the child to emulate. Obviously, the rewards don't have to be monetary. To be effective, they should be things that the child enjoys. As Ken Blanchard in his bestselling book *The One Minute Manager* says, "catch them doing something right." My wife home-schooled our three sons for several years. One of their favorite things is that she had a coupon reward system, where she gave them tickets for getting their lessons finished. Every week or two, the boys could redeem their tickets for items in a prize box, which had different price tags on them based on their cost. Even as adults, our sons look back at these memories as some of their fondest.

The second lesson is to connect choices with consequences. As adults, we like to control our kids and what happens to them. We make them obey us and in so doing, inadvertently curtail their ability to make decisions based on natural outcomes. A situation may go something like this. You want your 10-year-old to turn off television so that he can work on some schoolwork. "Ben, do as I told you right now. Turn off that TV and get to the table and study your math." Ben gets scolded several times and then grudgingly turns off the TV and drags his feet to the table, where he slams open his book, staring at the pages. But what if the next time you want Ben to study, you say, "Okay, you have two choices; you can keep watching TV for an hour, but if you choose that, you won't be able to watch TV for the next two days. Your favorite show is tomorrow, so you'd need to miss that. Or you can decide to finish your homework and then, if there's time left, you can watch some TV before bedtime and you can watch your show tomorrow. What choice do you want to make?"

Naturally, you hope Ben picks the second one, but you've given him power, the ability to choose. If he chooses to continue watching TV, then you need to stick to the no-TV for the next two days. When he objects, you non-emotionally remind him that he made the choice that resulted in no TV. I interviewed Scott Blanchard, the son of renowned leadership expert Ken Blanchard. Scott said, "I hated it when my parents disciplined me, because they'd always give me the talk. For example, if I got in trouble at school, the principal would call my parents. While most of my friends would get their car taken away or have to stay in the house for a week or so, I'd get "the talk." I'd come home and my dad would say, "Scott, have a seat." Then he'd ask, "What do you want to do in your life?" Scott said, "My mom and dad went to Cornell U., so I'd say, well, I want to go to Cornell U and be successful." Then his dad would ask, "So Scott, can you tell me how that decision you made at school today is going to help you accomplish those goals?" He said it was miserable, but it was the best thing. Scott said he uses the same principles with his kids now. By taking away choices from our kids, we dis-empower them, and when they become adults and get power, it will be more difficult for them to connect choices with consequences.

Naturally, you need to keep your child's safety in mind, but instead of losing your control and being physical with your children, you can have a decent conversation with them to help them understand the connection. This type of parenting is described in a book titled *Love and Logic*. So while this is a good parenting principle in general, it's essential for raising young leaders. Leader-oriented children like to feel that they have choices, because as leaders, they naturally want to decide. When we fail to give them a choice, we run the risk of frustrating them and not allowing them to develop self-discipline. When children have choices and experience consequences that aren't enjoyable, we help them learn self-discipline.

A third practice for raising self-disciplined children is increasing their responsibility as they prove themselves. Most things in life aren't defined by age limits, but rather by levels of responsibility. Some of these are age-oriented, which is why government sometimes intercedes for parents, but the big picture is that you want to equate freedom with responsibility. Regardless of age, the more a child demonstrates good choices and responsibility, the larger the decisions you can let them make. This reinforces the principle of choices and consequences. A child who fails to demonstrate self-discipline should be given fewer big choices. This prepares your child to function well as an adult, when you or a boss or authority figure are not present. Plus, it's a great way to prepare your child to lead because leaders possess the most authority in an organization and thus need to be self-disciplined.

A fourth practice is modeling self-discipline. It's difficult to teach what you don't practice. We make a greater impact with the lives we lead than the lessons we teach. Your life is a lesson. So if your child hears you gossiping about others, eating or drinking too much, or making unethical business deals, the examples they observe will certainly influence them to follow.

The ability to develop the muscle of self-discipline is one of the most important things parents can do for their children. It's important to all children, but essential for kids raised to lead.

Chapter 19

Growing a Problem Solver

Theme: Critical thinking is vital for leading and can be taught at an early age.

In the United States, companies have criticized schools for not turning out graduates equipped to be strong employees. As a result, in the last several years schools have started focusing on what we call 21st century skills. These include communication, collaboration, creativity, and critical thinking. The last one is about problem solving. Collaboration is about problem solving in a group. Much of what we teach in our KidLead training program is on leading problem-solving teams. In the classes I teach at USC on organizational behavior and leadership, we emphasize critical thinking and use case studies to help students solve real-life problems in organizations.

So how do you train children to be good problem solvers? Here are four vital steps to applying critical thinking.

First, help your child identify the causes of a problem. Research shows that adults would be more effective in solving problems if they invested more time on analyzing the problem. For example, revenues are down in a clothing company. The management team quickly decides they need to do more advertising and marketing. That may be true, but there could be other reasons behind the decline, such as a downturn in the economy, changing fashion trends, or competitors with lower prices and better quality. Depending on which problem is stronger, the solution will change. These are what we call root problems and fruit problems. A fruit problem is a symptom or side effect of a deeper issue, the root.

Let's put that in the context of teaching your child about decision making. Let's say your child is upset because another child wants to play with a toy she is using. The natural adult response is, "Jenna, let Kelsie play with the doll, too." That's a quick fix without helping the child identify the potential problem. Depending on the age of the child, a conversation could go something like this:

"Jenna, you seem upset that Kelsie wants to play with the doll. Is that because you started playing with the toy and are still having fun with it? Do you think it's that Kelsie can't find something to play with?" You begin by brainstorming potential issues, in this case only two or three, so as not to overwhelm the child. Eventually the child will be able to articulate her own ideas and then determine which is the stronger one. The selected problem determines what solution to employ. If the problem is that Jenna just started playing with the toy, it may be a time issue. If the problem is that Kelsie is bored, it's a lack of resources issue.

Second, facilitate thinking about potential solutions. Let's say Jenna thinks Kelsie is just bored and that she is looking for something to do.

You might say, "Let's think of three things you could do to help Kelsie find something to do. One might be if you invited her to play with you, sharing the doll. What's another idea?"

Jenna responds, "Well, I could help her find another doll."

"Good, good, that's two," you say. "What's one more thing you could do?"

"I guess I could see if she wanted to play with some other kids," Jenna offers.

Eventually, you can make a deal with your child that whenever she comes to you with a problem, she also needs to bring two possible solutions, requiring her to think for herself and depend on you less.

Third, analyze the strengths and benefits of each alternative to solving the problem. In other words, what are the pros and cons, the strengths and weaknesses, the benefits and risks? As children get older, this can be done more deeply, but the goal at this stage is to think critically. All solutions aren't the same. They have different strengths and weaknesses. So what might that look like in our illustration?

> "Jenna, what would be good about asking Kelsie to play with you?"
> —"We might have fun together and she'd stop bothering me."
> "What might <u>not</u> be good about asking Kelsie to play with you?"
> —"She might take the doll and then I wouldn't have it anymore."
> "True. What would be good if you found something else for Kelsie to play with?"
> —"She would be happy and then I could keep playing with the doll."
> "What might <u>not</u> be good about finding something else to play with?"
> —"It might take too much time and maybe she wouldn't want to do that."
> "True. What would be good if you asked some other kids to let Kelsie play with them?"
> —"She would be happy and not want my doll anymore."
> "What might <u>not</u> be good about asking other kids to let Kelsie play with them?"

—"They might not let her or she might not want to play with them."
"True."

Fourth, encourage your child to select the best solution and then implement it. By determining two or three alternatives, the child can now compare them and select the one she believes will work the best. This becomes the solution. But as we say in America, talk is cheap, so it's important to try and implement the solution while reducing the risks. Obviously, you need to use reason in terms of potential physical and emotional danger, but humans learn best by doing. By only talking about a solution, you withhold them from their strongest learning potential. It's important to help children experience consequences for their decisions. In this case, it might go like this.

"Jenna, which do you think is the best solution to this problem?"
—"I think I'll try to help Kelsie find a toy that she likes using, so that I can keep playing with the doll for awhile."
"Great, how could you do that and try to find something she'll like?"
—"I could ask her what else she likes doing and then offer to help her find it together, until I'm done playing with the doll."
"Excellent, why don't you go try that and let me know how it turns out."

Obviously, scripting an illustration like this sounds ideal, and in some ways it is, but by repeating processes like this over and over again, your child will create a pattern of thinking critically about solving problems that elevates the strongest solutions, resulting in the best outcomes. More importantly, you're training your child to think well on her own so that she doesn't need a parent, adult, or boss present to solve problems. This is helpful for all children, but essential if you want to raise a leader.

Chapter 20

How to Teach Like Socrates

Getting to leaders while they're moldable, not moldy!

Theme: The magic of asking strategic questions to catalyze your kid's thinking.

What are the most important life lessons you've learned from your parents and grandparents? How can you leave a legacy for your children? Those are pretty heavy duty questions, but they are examples of Socratic teaching because they require the student or audience to do more than merely listen. Adults are known for telling children what to think. We act like kids are empty buckets and our job is to pour into their heads whatever it is they need to know. But educational research shows us this isn't the best way to learn.

When we began investigating the best ways to develop young leaders, we looked at the most effective pedagogical methods. Experiential learning is the most potent, which is why we incorporate project-based methods into our training curriculum. But with it we add Socratic coaching during and after a mini-project. Although Socratic teaching involves more than merely asking questions, the questioning is one of the most unique things about this form of instruction.

The reason this approach is so successful with young leader training is that we want leaders who can think well. The good news is that you can learn how to tap into the magic of Socratic questioning whether or not you're striving to raise young leaders. When adults are answer-givers, we think we're helping our children, but really we aren't. It's more convenient for us to give answers to our children, but it's a lazy approach. Plus we feel superior because we know things they do not. The ancient proverb says, "Give a man a fish; feed him for a meal. Teach him to fish; feed him for life." The reason Socratic questioning is so important in the development of young leaders is we want to equip them to think like leaders when adult authority figures are not present. We want them to be able to think for themselves, not just do what they're told.

So what does it take to use Socratic questioning in developing our children and youth?

First, identify teachable moments. If you read the preceding chapter, you may remember the story I told about Ken Blanchard and his son, Scott. This is an example of Socratic questioning in terms of helping a child learn self-discipline. A teachable moment is a situation when you have the opportunity to assist the child in learning about a life lesson. Typically, it could be a question the child asks about something that requires more than a simple answer, such as "Why is Jenny so mean?" or "Why do you make me pick up my toys before I go to bed?" or "What do you think I should take for Show-and-Tell at school?" While children often don't initiate questions, more common situations involve issues such as eating healthy foods at mealtime, going to bed on time, turning off video games, doing homework, and relational issues like sharing toys, responding nicely to peers who are overbearing, and other conflict issues.

A teachable moment also involves a time issue. Typically, you need to respond Socratically immediately with young children (ages 3-6). The older a child gets, the more you can delay Socratic questioning to a time that's more convenient, so long as it's not too long. The best approach is to not wait more than 24 hours, even with teens.

Second, turn the answer into a question. The United States has a game show called Jeopardy. It's a challenge where contestants are given answers, and then they have to respond to them by giving a question that matches the answer. Socratic questioning is a bit like that. You need to know the answer, but then turn it into a question where the child can think about the answer. This helps the child think at a deeper level than merely listening to the adult tell them what to think. For example, if a child asks, "Why do I need to do my homework now?" instead of answering, "Because I said so," you might ask, "Why do you think it's important to do the assignments that your teacher expects?" You may need to pause a moment or two to come up with the appropriate question, but it's better than simply giving the child your version of the answer.

Third, go deeper. When you begin the process of Socratic questioning, sometimes you feel satisfied with the first response. But effective teaching frequently goes multiple rounds, meaning that you will need to think of more involved questions to keep the thinking going. Children, like all of us, can be cognitive misers. We don't always feel like thinking, because it's hard work. Consider the brain like a muscle. It takes exercise to strengthen it. You could even turn it into a game, such as "Three Questions." That way it forces you to ask productive questions but lets them know it won't last forever.

For example, if a child hits a friend for taking his toy, you might say: "Let's play Three Questions. Question 1: What were you trying to accomplish by hitting Brian?"

Your child says, "I hit him to let him know I was mad at him for taking my ball."

"Question 2: What might have been another way to let Brian know you were mad at him?"

"I could tell him."

"Question 3: How might telling him be better than hitting him next time?"

"I wouldn't get in trouble that way."

So even though this may not be a prolonged conversation, at least you've created a simple format for elevating awareness and helping your child think more deeply about his or her actions.

Naturally, every situation doesn't lend itself to Socratic question asking. If a child is about to run into a street to fetch a ball, you're not going to ask questions. You're going to scream, "Stop! Don't run into the street." (Although after the emergency is over, you can delve into important Socratic discussion.) Older children are better at remembering events that you can debrief with them. Young children tend to live in the present, so conversations after-the-fact tend to be less productive. When you begin thinking Socratically, you'll discover more opportunities to teach that way than you have the time. Sometimes you don't have the patience, or the child doesn't have the energy to participate. Yet because there are so many opportunities every day to engage in Socratic questioning, certainly you can find times throughout the week to employ this powerful teaching method.

Like all practices, both you and your child will get used to using them and they'll become second nature. The interesting thing is that as friends and family members see you using these strategies, they'll at first be intrigued and occasionally critical, but the attitude and behavior of your children will eventually impress them with your parenting methods.

So while Socratic questioning is a great method to employ for all kids, it's very important for raising young leaders who like to feel empowered and who need to learn how to think critically—not just respond to authority figures telling them what to do.

Chapter 21

Home Leadership Projects

Theme: Creating leadership development activities with your family.

Leaders, leading, and leadership are all around us. The beauty of that is you can tap into everyday routines and events to develop your child's potential in this area. We've discussed how to develop your home into a leader incubator. I also gave you a sample project of overseeing a meal team. But now let's take that a step further and give you four more project examples that you can do in your home. Before we do that, let me remind you of the three basic ingredients for an authentic leadership training project.

First, there needs to be a team of at least three people. This makes the focus on leading, not just doing chores alone. Second, there should be a clear goal. The outcome should be determined, but not the process. That's a part of the leader's responsibility. What is the end goal you want to achieve? Third, there need to be resources and risks. These go together, whether they be time, money, or other things, so that the leader can make actual decisions that result in potential success or failure.

The first project I'd like to suggest is organizing a room. By room organizing I mean cleaning, redecorating, or rearranging things. This could be the child's room, a storage or playroom, a garage, or another designated living space that allows a child to oversee a team of others who are organizing it. They could be family members, friends, or classmates. You may even want to promise a treat or reward when the task is adequately completed, after inspection, of course.

The conversation could go something like this:

Parent: *Bree, I don't know if you've noticed, but our storage room has become very disorganized and cluttered. I'd like to put you in charge of getting it organized. I'm not asking you to do it yourself. In fact, you can't do it alone. You need to lead a team of two other people who'll clean and organize it and make it nicer to use and be in. Do you think you can do that?*

Bree: *So, you mean I don't have to do it myself?*

Parent: *That is correct. We want you to be the leader. You need to recruit at least two others and supervise them, helping them know what to do.*

Bree: *What if I don't know where something goes or like what to do with all those clothes in the corner?*

Parent: *Well, like all leaders, you can ask for advice. Being a leader doesn't mean you have all the answers, but you get information and then help make the final decision.*

Bree: *So who would I get on the team?*

Parent: *That's up to you. It could be me, Dad, your brother, or even a couple of friends. Plus, after you're done, as soon as I approve of the job you did, I'll let you have that sleepover you've been wanting.*

So that's one project idea. A second project I'd like to suggest is a day-off trip. The goal of this is to let your child determine what you do, where you go, and again, who will be on the trip. Naturally, you can specify resources, including time, money, and risk. The opportunity for a child to decide what you're going to do, how you're going to get there, how much it will cost, and negotiating potential priority conflicts with team members have a lot to do with leading at all ages.

The possibilities could include a trip to the mall, the zoo, a favorite park or beach, a movie, and even larger ticket items such as overnight in a nearby city and amusement park. Figure out beforehand what limitations you want to put on the event, but other than that, make sure you allow the child to truly lead, even if it isn't your favorite way to spend your money or time off from work.

A third leadership project you can do at home is for your child to plan and lead a shopping trip. Even though you do these every week, with a little planning you can tap into the process and help your child develop his or her leadership potential. Whether you're grocery shopping, looking for school clothes, or hunting for new furnishings, these can be wonderful opportunities to develop organizational skills. The process will require more work for you in that you'll need to pre-think your budget, what you want or need to acquire, and potential challenges of letting your child make decisions.

Among these options, grocery shopping may be the most productive because food is less permanent and therefore less likely to be frustrating if disappointing decisions are made. Again, figure out how you'll make this a team event so that you consider what is needed, including a budget, and who is going to look for what in the store. Perhaps it's as simple as Mom, Dad, and child walking the aisles and letting the child decide on what does and does not go into cart. How will you get to the store? When will it happen? How much do you have to spend? Who'll bring the groceries into the house? Who will put them away?

A fourth project idea for your child is to create a family game. Playing games as a family is one of the best ways to create memories that last a lifetime. Most families are familiar with board games and informal make-believe play. This project idea falls somewhat in the middle. The goal is for a child to lead the family in creating a new game concept, with rules, roles, and outcomes. You may even want to assist the challenge by selecting three to six objects, such as a chair, paper, wastebasket, paper clips, and umbrella. Then ask the child to lead the team in coming up with a game that uses all of those resources. I'd avoid including balls, since this often makes it too easy and less creative. The game should be fun, easy to learn, and different from other games. Pretend that a toy company has asked the child to lead a team of game makers to design a fun game based on these items.

After you come up with the game, make sure you play it to see how it went and what improvements you might make. A great way to celebrate this is to ask your child to lead the game in another setting with other people, so she or he can see the results and be honored as a young leader.

So there you have four leadership development project ideas you can use at home. After each one, make sure you take time to sit down and discuss how things went. Here are some potential debrief questions to consider:

- What did you like about being the leader?
- What did you not enjoy about being the leader?
- Who seemed to do well on your team?
- Who seemed to struggle on your team?
- What would you do differently next time?

Go deeper on any of these questions by saying things such as "Tell me more" and "Help me understand..." and "Can you give me another example of that?" These and similar comments help your child think more deeply about the activity. As you can see, you can turn everyday home opportunities into ways to develop the leadership potential of your child.

Chapter 22

Community Leadership Projects

Theme: Creating leadership development activities for your child in the neighborhood.

I just finished grading papers for a class of my MBA students at the University of California Irvine. These are team projects where they did an organizational analysis, involving interviews and site visits of a company. They did well, but frequently they'd make statements in their reports where in my comments I'd write, "Give me an example." A specific story provides support behind a concept and illustrates how this actually happens and what you mean.

In the previous chapter I gave you four examples of leadership projects you can do with your family, related to your home life. I'm confident they will inspire many more project ideas. In this chapter, I'd like to offer four more examples of leadership development projects outside your home, involving other people. These will help you bring the concepts we've been talking about in this book to life.

But first, let me remind you of the three basic ingredients for an authentic leadership training project.

First, there needs to be a team of at least three people. This makes the focus on leading, not just doing chores alone. Second, there should be a clear goal. The focus is on the outcome, not the process. What is the end outcome you want to achieve? Third, there need to be resources and risks. These go together, whether they be time, money, or other things, so the leader can make decisions that result in potential success or failure.

Okay, here's the first project idea. I call it Good Deed Day. This project is in your neighborhood and involves your child leading two or more in doing an act of kindness for other people. Part of the fun of this is brainstorming ideas. This gets your child into thinking about others. Self-centeredness is a human nature issue; most people think more about themselves than others. Children wrestle with this a lot. But instead of telling people to care more, it's often more effective to do something to help others, creating a sense of charitability. Most of the time, helping others makes us feel good. Good Deed Day could become an annual, quarterly, or even bi-monthly event that your child does. Good deeds could be things such as cleaning a vacant lot in your area where trash has collected. It could involve baking cookies, wrapping them up, and taking them to neighbors. Another good deed might involve creating "Have a nice day!" cards and then passing them out to people who walk by your street or letting your child give them to people at your work. Again, the key is to assist the child in coming up with his or her own idea and making sure she or he leads a team of at least two others in the process.

Another idea is a charity support event. Chances are you'll need to do some work ahead of time to identify one or two organizations near you that help people. We call these non-profits in the United States. Nearly all non-profits I know need the assistance of volunteers periodically or all the time. By scouting for ideas and potential projects, you can suggest a few to your child who will then pick the one she or he thinks is good. Then the child's job as the leader is to recruit people to go to the charity together and work as a team on a project. It could even be a project done in your neighborhood that supports the charity.

For example, if the charity gives clothes to the poor, perhaps your child gets the team to encourage others to donate clothes they don't use, collect them, and then take them to the charity. If the non-profit gives food, perhaps it is doing the same but gathering food to donate.

If the charity is doing a fundraiser, then it may need volunteers to work the event. Your child can recruit a team that does that. It could involve setting up a table outside of a store or business and handing out flyers to encourage people to donate items. Since most charities are looking for support from volunteers, projects like these are readily available. The fact that a child is leading a team of volunteers is impressive and will no doubt be used as an example for others who may want to help the non-profit.

A third neighborhood project idea to develop your child's leadership potential is an entrepreneurial mini-business. This could be as simple as a lemonade or cold-water stand, selling drinks to people walking by your home or neighborhood. It could be selling cookies door to door, either homemade or purchased in the store and packaged into smaller portions. A service project might involve walking pets, washing windows, or doing lawn care. When our middle son was a teen, he started his own service company called Bro Mow. He hired his younger brother and they went around our neighborhood passing out flyers, offering to mow the grass in people's yards. My wife and I were on call in case we needed to drive them and the lawnmower.

Bro Mow became a snow shoveling company in the winter. Because they built rapport with people, they were even hired at times to walk pets and pick up mail and newspapers when the neighbors went on vacation. The boys made quite a bit of money with this little company of theirs. Obviously, there was conflict at times as the younger brother questioned why he didn't get paid as much as his older brother, but this too became an opportunity to manage conflict and look at the issue of economics and budgets. In addition, they learned the work ethic and issues related to marketing, setting prices, interacting with customers, and costs. Your child could recruit a team to come up with the concepts, create a strategy, and design signage.

A fourth neighborhood project idea involves helping senior citizens. Even though this is related to the Good Deed Day and could also be a project with a non-profit charity, nearly every community has a need to care for and encourage older people. Other countries do this better than the United States, where many senior citizens live alone or in communities, but most older people appreciate being around children. What this does for your child is make them feel comfortable around the aged and gives them a sense of purpose and generosity. The project could be as simple as getting a small team to visit a senior citizen who lives alone. It might involve offering to do little household tasks or just sit with the person in her living room and talk. My wife is the executive director of an upscale senior living facility in Calabasas, California. It costs a lot of money to live there, and thus most of the families are somewhat wealthy. Yet the residents love when people, especially children and youth, come to visit them. There's just something about young people that seniors love. Projects like these teach your child to honor the aged and serve others.

So there you have four leadership project ideas you can use in your community. After each one, make sure you take time to discuss how things went. Here are some potential debrief questions:

- What did you like about being the leader?
- What did you not enjoy about being the leader?
- Who seemed to do well on your team?
- Who seemed to struggle on your team and why?
- What would you do differently next time?

Go deeper on any of these question by saying things such as "Tell me more," and "Help me understand..." and "Can you give me another example of that?" These and similar comments help your child think more deeply about the activity. As you can see, opportunities to develop your child's leadership potential are all around you.

Chapter 23
Finding a Leader Mentor

Theme: Who, how, and where to look for someone who'll mentor your young leaders.

The word *mentor*, at least the English version of the term, comes from an ancient Greek epic poem by Homer called the "Odyssey." Mentor was a friend of Odysseus and adviser of Telemachus. The name is based on the word *mentos*, meaning intent, purpose, spirit, and passion. It is also rooted in the word meaning "to think," as in mental activity. So the basic background of a mentor is an adviser who makes us think. Specifically, in our context here, a mentor is an adult leader who can speak into the life of a protégé, namely a child or youth. The word *protégé* means one who is protected, so a mentor can protect a future leader from wrong concepts about leading and using power and influence irresponsibly.

The primary goal of a mentor is not to tutor or coach. Rather, it is to offer a context for leading and wisdom. Whether it is a one-time event or an ongoing, formal relationship, a mentor helps a young person think differently about what it means to lead. It is a way of speeding up the process by modeling leading and transferring wisdom from generation to generation. There are two primary and two secondary benefits of finding a mentor for your child or teen.

The first major benefit is the esteem and honor that an older leader can offer a child. The social connection between a mentor and your child can make a lifetime impact. Taking pictures, notes, and reviewing interactions can build a young leader's confidence. This alone is a significant ingredient to developing leaders at an early age. You're giving them a big head start.

A second major benefit for your child is to learn from someone other than a parent or teacher, specifically focusing on leadership. An athletic coach instructs on a specific physical skill. Teachers emphasize intellectual abilities. But a leader will help catalyze the leadership potential in a child, especially if this type of talent is identified. Imagine a budding golfer spending the day with Tiger Woods, or a young basketball phenom getting personal advice from Yao Ming. This impact can elevate the vision of a child who possesses a high capacity to lead.

A secondary benefit for your child is if the mentor extends an opportunity for the young leader to interact with him or her during staff meetings or as an intern. Although this would need to come as an invitation from the leader, many older leaders see themselves in kids and youth with a high capacity to lead. They feel a kinship with them so that if they enjoy their initial interaction, they may want to prolong it with other mentoring opportunities.

Another secondary benefit is related to the first, but it has to do with future networking. Once a young leader connects with a veteran leader, that leader can open future doors, from university recommendations to job opportunities. Don't underestimate the potential in building rapport with an influential mentor.

So how do you find a person who could mentor your child? Begin with your network. Consider a proven leader in the organization where you work. Think about people you know who are connected with other people. The power of networking is not just who you know but the people known by those you know. Granted, the younger the age of the child, the more you'll need a personal relationship to recruit a mentor. It's easier to connect a mentor with an older teen than an eight-year-old. But don't let that stop you from looking for a possible mentor for a preteen. I've introduced each of our sons to several influential people, from simple introductions to employment opportunities.

If and when you have an idea of who you'd like to invite as your child's mentor, consider your pitch. I've found that very few leaders establish official mentoring relationships. One of the reasons is that they're so busy. Another is that, believe it or not, they don't feel confident in establishing a mentoring role. Unless the leader has a small child himself or herself, there's a natural intimidation factor in terms of, "What would I do or say?" This concern can be reduced if you simply make the event a half-day shadowing, much like a take-your-child-to-work day. Most leaders are honored to be asked, yet rarely are, because most people are intimidated. An ancient spiritual leader once said, "You have not, because you ask not." No one likes being rejected, and many assume that a veteran leader would have no time for a child. That's not necessarily true. If you suggest little more than allowing the child to observe the leader during meetings, seeing the office and sitting in his or her chair, there would be little to no extra work. You could even offer to chaperone the child if the leader seems unsure.

If you complete a leadership assessment on your child like the NYLI and the score reveals an elevated probability of leadership giftedness, meaning a score of 3.8 or more, you can mention that in your request. If the leader perceives that this isn't just a regular child but rather one identified as potentially gifted in leadership, there's a greater chance the leader will relate to the young person. Remember, every great leader was at one time a 12-year-old. Suggest the value of investing in future leaders and creating a low-level commitment. You want to make it easy for the mentor to say yes.

If the leader seems unsure of what to do or how to interact with your child, you can provide some of these ideas and questions:

* Let the child simply follow you around on a normal day's schedule.
* Describe what you like about being a leader.
* Explain what you don't enjoy about leading or what makes it difficult.
* Talk about when you started to think about yourself as a leader.
* Was there a person who mentored you or seemed to recognize your

leadership ability?
* What advice would you give to a young leader?

If your child hesitates, consider offering her some of the following questions to ask the mentor. You can even have her write these on a card or pad of paper, where she can also take notes.
* How old were you when you thought you might have leadership ability?
* What do you look for in young leaders?
* What do you like and dislike about leading?
* What have you learned from your failures?
* What do you now know that you wish you knew when you began as a leader?
* What advice would you give a person like me, who wants to learn how to lead?

After the event, take time to sit with your child and discuss the various activities, what she saw and what it felt like to meet the leader.
Naturally, send a gracious thank-you note from yourself and your child.
Then, if it seems to fit, consider following up with other opportunities.
This could be something as simple as a similar meeting in 6-12 months.
If the leader enjoyed himself in the process, this could encourage him to follow up. The idea of an executive mentoring future leaders is a feel-good experience, plus it's a great public relations opportunity.

Establishing a few guidelines is important for most potential mentors.
There's also a concern these days about negative public relations and legal concerns regarding being alone with a minor. You may need to be ready to address these issues beforehand. But these should be low barriers to overcome, given the high level of benefits of finding a mentor for your child. Assisting your child in establishing mentoring relationships with adult leaders is a powerful developmental tool.

Chapter 24

Leading Up

Theme: Training your child on how to influence those with more power.

When our children were young, they liked eating at McDonald's. I remember on more than one occasion, while driving the family van, my wife and I decided we didn't want to go there. Yet through our sons' persuasive voices, we eventually ended up in the McDonald's drive-through lane. What had happened? I was driving the van. I had more power and control than they did. But they had learned how to lead up. Obviously, all kids learn ways to influence their parents and certainly their grandparents. But let me talk about how this relates to "leading up" and then offer ways to introduce this to your child.

In organizational behavior, we talk about power and influence. Power is the potential to have influence, and influence is power-activated. Influence is dynamic, meaning it is fluid and is somewhat difficult to contain or predict. Power is available through several sources. In organizations, we often think of power coming from a position of authority, such as a manager or the CEO. But actually there are several other sources of power, such as information: the knowledge you have about a process or person. Another resource is referent power, focusing on a person's charm and personality, as well as people you know in your network. Still other power sources include resources, such as money, physical strength, or in the context of a country, military capability. Another type of power is expertise, referring to talent, skill, and experience in a specific area. For example, people who possess exceptional talent in software programming possess power when organizations need this type of expertise.

The reason I describe these types of power sources is for you to help your child know that just because he or she is not the boss, that doesn't mean they don't possess power. Throughout history, people who did not hold positions of high authority have accomplished incredible things through others. Because young leaders rarely occupy positions of authority, they need to use other means to get things done. In the world of business, there's a term called OPM; that stands for Other People's Money. Investors, who may not have enough of their own capital, can use other people's money to make profits. In the world of leadership, we use OPI, or Other People's Influence.

Most books on leadership focus on leading down, referring to people on your team who report to you. Among the 700 books on leadership I had in my library at one time, over 98% focused on leading down. But young leaders, to be successful, need to learn how to lead up. They need to know how to influence those who possess power to get things done. Depending on the age of your child and your child's natural leadership aptitude, you'll need to express these ideas in ways they can understand. Naturally, the older a child is and the higher the natural leadership talent, the faster the child will catch on to these ideas. Yet, even children without strong leadership ability can learn to tap into other people's influence through these practices. Believe it or not, it may even give you a few ideas of how you can increase your influence with your superiors at work.

First, try to explain the idea of influence through concrete ways. For example, I told the simple story of how my kids influenced me to go McDonald's even though I was the one driving the van. Think of two or three stories like these that you can tell your child. Break these down and talk about positive and negative ways to influence others. Positive examples of influence would be if your child asks you nicely to go to McDonald's; or suggests that if she gets food at McDonald's, you could get food somewhere else; or she promises to clean her room as soon as you got home from McDonald's.

Negative ways of influence would be if she cried and screamed and was disrespectful. People with power don't like to help others when they try to get them to do things using negative tactics.

Next, try to come up with some examples of people who have more power than your child. Some of the more natural ones may be a teacher, a coach, or a friend's parent. Then brainstorm ways the child can influence that person to use their power in a way that would help the child accomplish her goal. For example, the conversation might go like this:

"Jessica, your mom and I have a boss at work. Our bosses have more power than we do, so we often need to do what they ask, but that doesn't mean we're powerless. We know how to help them give us what we need, too. Who is like a boss to you, besides your mom and me?"

Jessica responds, "Well, my teacher, Mrs. Gray, is like that."

"Good, that's right, she is," you say. "What do you think you could do to get Mrs. Gray to be more on your side at school?"

"Well, I could do what she asks and not talk to my friends during class," Jessica says.

"Good, good, what else?"

"Well, she likes flowers, so maybe I could bring her a flower in a vase for her desk."

"Good, I like that. Let's think of one more thing you could do."

"Well, I could ask her if there were any chores she needed help with, such as taking out the trash or washing the whiteboards."
"Excellent," you say. "Leaders like it when we figure out ways to help them accomplish their goals. Now, can you think of what your teacher could do for you that requires her power to do it?"

"Hmm, well, sometimes I like getting a pass to go to the library, but usually she says 'no' because she wants to keep us all together in the class. She's afraid I'll get in trouble or something."

"Okay, so after you do some of these things to help your teacher, then you can politely ask her for a pass to go to the library and then we'll see what happens and talk about it. That may be a way you can use her power, by using your influence of being kinder and more responsible than the other kids."

This is an example of a starter conversation. Continue to discuss things like this to empower children and youth with ways they can lead up and tap other people's power. The ability to influence influencers is one of the most overlooked techniques in gaining power to accomplish what you're striving to achieve. As a parent, you can also use this strategy, along with Socratic coaching, to help your child be more effective at influencing you. That's right, in teaching her how to influence you as parents, you're actually equipping her with great organizational skills related to power.

Sometimes we let our old mental recordings get in the way of how we raise our kids. A lot of parents act like a bossy boss with their kids. Usually it's because that's the way their parents did it. You have an opportunity to interrupt tradition and improve parenting practices, not to make your kids your friends like many do these days, but rather to help them understand how the world works. When people possess higher levels of power, there are effective ways for those with less power to still influence. That's what we call leading up.

Chapter 25

Sideways Leading

Theme: Social banking and influencing peers.

I was quite surprised on my first visit to China, because sometimes we Americans think we are ahead of everyone else in the world. This kind of pride can be debilitating. One of the things I noticed is how far behind we are in the area of commerce technology. Most people in the U.S. rely heavily on credit and debit cards. Only recently has cell phone technology started to become a common practice in buying and selling. In fact, certain demographics still rely primarily on cash. But in China, nearly everyone I saw was buying and selling using their smart phones. I discovered that I couldn't purchase food in some places because they only used cell phone technology. But whether you use a plastic card or cell phone to make purchases, you still need to have money in your bank account.

I'm going to use banking as a metaphor to explain lateral leadership, in hopes that you can explain this to your young leader. In the previous chapter we discussed leading up, which focuses on influencing people who possess more power than you. This is important for children and youth because until they get older, chances are they'll have less power than those they work around. Yet there are ways they can get things done using other people's power. At the same time, they need to learn how to lead laterally, meaning those who have similar power to them. This could be a sibling, friends at school, or eventually colleagues at work. While most books on leadership focus on leading down, referring to those who report to you, leading up and leading laterally are just as important for leaders while they're young.

So let's get back to the banking metaphor to help explain how to influence people around you. This can be used to explain leading up and leading down, but it's probably most useful in terms of learning how to lead among peers and others who share similar levels of power.

Think of a person as a bank. When you establish a relationship with another person, it's like you're opening an account with <u>your</u> name on it in <u>their bank</u>. At the same time, that person is opening up an account with their name on it in your bank. If you want to take money out of your bank, you need to make deposits. For example, if you want to buy a sweater that costs $50, you need to have at least $50 in your bank account. But if you try to buy a $100 sweater and you only have $50 in your account, your bank will block the transaction and the store owner will say, "I'm sorry, you don't have enough money in your account to purchase it."

If you want to buy that $100 sweater, you need to make a deposit to increase your balance. The same is true in our relationships with others. The way we make deposits is by being kind, complimenting the other person, doing your work, and communicating well. These are all examples of earning social credits. When you have sufficient credits in your account in the other person's bank, then you can make withdrawals. A withdrawal is when someone does something for you. It could also be when you intentionally or accidentally offend or disappoint them. These subtract from your balance.

For example, let's say that you begin a relationship with a new person at work. Initially, you have a cordial conversation and decide to eat lunch together. You welcome your new colleague to the department and you wonder if the other person could become a friend. The next day, the new person asks for your help in getting acclimated to her computer, logging into her account, and some other things related to being new.

Even though she's gone through the Human Relations training of a new employee, you willingly help her anyway. Next week, the new employee asks you to help her do a couple of her work assignments. Even though you're busy with your own projects, you interrupt your work to help. This goes on for a few weeks, so much that you begin feeling resentful. This person you befriended now seems to be using you. She says "Thank you," but doesn't seem overly appreciative. The next week, when she asks you for a favor, you respond, "You know, I have so much work of my own, I can't help you this time." The woman seems to be offended and says, "Well I didn't know it was such a big deal. Don't worry, I'll ask someone else." You walk away, angry at her ungrateful response. The new employee seems to ignore you over the next few days, making you even more frustrated that you were so kind to her at the start.

What happened in this scenario? We've all experienced it, when a relationship seems to be one-sided. Going back to our metaphor, it's the equivalent of being overdrawn in your bank account, so that the bank no longer lets you buy things and even puts a hold on your account. When husbands and wives decide to divorce, it's because one or both have overdrawn their social bank accounts and decide to close their accounts. Sometimes, when one person seems to be overly patient, it's because she's offering credit to the other person. Credit is when the bank loans us money, assuming we will pay it back with interest. But like a cash account, credit has limits. When you're overextended, your relationship with the bank ends or worse, starts legal action.

If your child is a teen, chances are he or she will be able to understand this analogy. You can discuss this in terms of listing a few friends or peers and then brainstorming actions that are deposits. Then ask for ideas on what actions or responses might be considered withdrawals, or subtractions. The idea of leadership is that leaders try to get things done with these social credits, not just let them sit in the bank without drawing interest or investing them. Leaders need to have a good estimate of how many social credits are in the bank, and how to create more, before making a big withdrawal. If you want someone at school to be on your team instead of someone else's, it may help if you've established a relationship first and then built a balance in your social bank account.

Because metaphors are conceptual, this may be more difficult to use with kids under 12, because until then they're primarily concrete thinkers and have more difficulty with concepts. Here's an idea of conveying this concept tangibly. You can get two jars, one with your name on it and the other with your child's name. You can add jars for other people. Get a large number of beans and place them in a bag. I'd avoid actual money, because you don't want to convey the idea of buying good behavior or paying for love. Rather, you can use this as a teaching program for a month. When your child does something nice, obeys you, works in the kitchen, or cleans his room, then you add beans to his jar. At the same time, you ask your child to put beans in your jar when you play with him, help him with his school work, or come home from work early to spend time with the family.

Then, if your child doesn't do his homework, clean his room, or perhaps wants to watch a bit more TV than usual, you can ask him to take an appropriate number of beans out of his jar. These go back into the storage bag. Explain that when you do things that disappoint each other, it reduces the amount in each other's jars. Then it's time to figure out how to add more, in case you want a special favor. Although simple, this can teach a powerful principle of influencing those around us, which is what we refer to as leading laterally.

Chapter 26

Dealing with Bullies

Theme: Teaching children to tackle bullying from a leadership perspective.

Kevin Akers was an older neighbor boy who picked on me (and other kids) as we rode the bus to school. Every Monday through Friday, at 7:15 a.m., a big yellow school bus stopped in front of our farmhouse to take me to school. Two or three stops later, we picked up the Aker boys. The youngest was about my age, but the older brother, Kevin, was 4 or 5 years older. He was a troublemaker. Kevin would sit near the back of the bus, so most kids tried to avoid him. But sometimes, mostly on the bus ride home from school, Kevin would walk back and randomly decide who he wanted to pick on that day. Sometimes he'd pull your ear or your hair. Other times he'd put his fist in front of your face or call you names. Everyone hated it. Kevin was our local bully.

Bullies and bullying are hot topics in society today. People are tired of individuals who use their strength and power to intimidate others, making them feel small and creating fear. These real and perceived threats can cause long-term pain.

I don't claim to be an authority on bullying, but I do understand the difference between an individual bully and a bully who is a leader. Sometimes I hear people say things such as, "Bullies are terrible leaders." Actually, that's not necessarily true. There are individual bullies and there are leader bullies. A bully who picks on others by himself is not a leader. She or he is often a loner, with few or no friends. The lone bully is a sad and angry person with unresolved issues caused by home life, abuse, or even chemical imbalances.

An interesting thing about children possessing leadership ability is a willingness to stand up to bullies. This is an early indicator, standing against perceived injustices. In this case, leaders feel comfortable with power and bullies wield power, even if it is coercive. Another reason leader-oriented children are more willing than others to step up to bullies is they possess a sense of justice combined with a willingness to confront things that seem unfair. Sometimes they get in trouble for taking this risk, because they'll stand up to a teacher, principal, coach, or parent if they feel like a rule, policy, or practice is not right. A final reason kids with leadership talent are more willing to confront bullies is their concern for others. This social awareness compels them to stand up to a bully, but it can also get them hurt.

But let's talk about the biggest danger in society: a bully who is also a leader. The reason is that this mean person is good at recruiting others to join him in bullying. As a teen and young adult, it may involve leading a youth gang. Some bullies grow out of their negative behavior, but others become adult bullies who win by intimidation and take advantage of people. If you look at history, you can see that many world leaders are basically bully leaders because they get so many others to follow them in hurting people and creating fear. Terrorism is an example of bullies led by bully leaders.

A bully leader often uses her leadership to recruit and empower followers, inspiring them to use coercion to intimidate others. Some might look at Adolf Hitler and say he wasn't really a leader; I disagree. He was a leader among many of his committed followers, but he used coercion to gain compliance from others. That's why these types of people are so dangerous in organizations and society at large.

The problem is that no amount of proactive strategies are going to remove every bully from school busses, playgrounds, neighborhoods, corporations, and governments. It is a social issue occurring through history. The good news is that we can reduce the number of bully leaders by identifying those with leadership talent early and then intentionally shaping their character. That is one of the core reasons I started KidLead, to get to leaders while they're moldable, not moldy. Our goal isn't just to help kids become great leaders. It's also to get to potentially evil leaders early, to change their character while it's still pliable.

What can you do to help your child handle bullying? Education needs to be done at your child's age level. One of the best strategies is to facilitate Socratic conversations, asking your child why she or he thinks the bully is behaving that way. Some potential questions might include:

- When is a person being a bully?
- What does a bully say or do to hurt others?
- Why do you think this person does it?
- Do you think it may be because he is sad? How do you respond when you are sad?
- Do you think it may be because he is angry? How do you respond when you are angry?
- I think people are sometimes bullies because that's how their mom or dad treated them. That's how they think they should act. Why do you think this person responds this way?
- I think people are sometimes bullies because they want attention. How does being a bully get attention? Is this good or bad attention?
- Do you think this person could be nice?
- What do you think it would take to help this person be nicer?

Questions like these help identify the concept of bullying and educate children on what is behind the behavior. The next step is to assist your child in coming up with ways to respond to a bully.

- One strategy is to ignore the bully. This means physically as well as virtually, online, where bullying is growing the fastest. Take a different path from school, block the person from your social media, and don't respond to bullying comments.

- Another response is to report the bully to an authority figure, such as a parent, teacher, or coach. Although the risk of this is being seen as a wimp or tattle-tale, it's more effective than doing nothing.
- A third option is to develop a coalition of friends, peers who will stick up for each other if any one of them is in a situation with a bully. There is power in numbers. A group can intimidate the bully, who often focuses on weaker individuals.
- A fourth option is counter-intuitive; befriend the bully. The goal is not to become a part of the bully's entourage, if the bully is also a leader. Rather, the goal is to use social banking that we discussed in the last chapter. This can be done by being complimentary, talking to the bully, sharing a joke or story, and finding out more about him. They yearn for attention. Negative attention is better than no attention in their minds. The reason is that bullies often lack self-esteem and dignity. Their bullying gives them a sense of importance, even if distorted. Someone said, "Keep your friends close, but keep your enemies closer."

Although bullying will never be extinguished, we can help our children learn to be more effective with them as well as helping our children who are leaders never become bullies.

Chapter 27

To Follow or Not to Follow

Theme: Teaching children how to identify good and bad leaders.

I'm convinced that it's possible to see great leaders, even when they're very young. It's important to begin developing those with organizational abilities at an early age, to give them a big head start and shape their character for the good.

But whether your child is gifted in leadership or not, you want to make sure that he or she can distinguish good leaders from bad ones. Throughout history, people who did not understand the process of leadership and were unable to discern evil leaders got caught up into doing terrible things. Remember, a person who is leading without followers is merely taking a walk. The best way to thwart the power of an evil leader is to stop following him. To be a leader, you must have people who follow you.

Here are some practical ideas to help your child distinguish good leaders from bad ones. If your child has leadership talent, then this will be even more helpful because it will provide a model of what you want her to become and a clear picture of what you don't want her to be.

First, discuss good and bad leaders Socratically. For example, let's say at mealtime your child tells you about a student who got in trouble for throwing food. Some of your questions may go like this:

- Why do you think Benji threw the food?
- Did other kids begin throwing food after Benji started?
- What happened when he got in trouble?
- Do other kids often follow Benji at school?
- Why do you think they follow him?
- Is he a good leader or not a good leader?
- Why is it important to follow only good leaders?

Questions liked these, brought up in conversational, non-judgmental tones, allow a child or teen to think more clearly about qualities. You don't need to lecture, criticize, or say things such as "Make sure you stay away from Benji." Rather, help your

child make good choices based on what he learns. The more you practice this skill, the better you'll get at directing conversations without lecturing or giving pat answers.

Another way to begin discussions on good and bad leaders is when you watch television or movies where you see both types depicted. Most storylines have heroes and villains. Look for examples where the good and bad people are leaders, meaning others are following them. This lets you talk about the ability leaders possess to attract others to them and then how they guide them for good or bad, along with the results.

A third thing to consider is who spends time with your child. Although you can't always pick your child's friends, you can certainly influence who they see, and how often and how long they interact with them. Much of this has to do with parenting values and styles of other families. If you know the adults of the family don't reflect your standards, then try to avoid letting your children spend much time with them. This is especially important if the other children are older or leader-oriented. Conversely, if you know of kids who are strong, positive leaders, then do what you can to recruit them to play with your child and spend time together. A proverb says, "Bad company corrupts good character."

Along with this, consider who takes care of your children. When our children were young, we did our best to help them have strong caregivers when we needed to be away. Because we didn't live near any of our parents or relatives, it meant we needed to think about responsibility and character, not just availability. One of our caregivers, Charlette, taught our sons French while she supervised them. Her fun, positive attitude provided a good example of an ambitious young person. After high school she attended Cornell University.

Another caregiver our boys liked was a teen named Jeff DeWit. Jeff conveyed strong leadership qualities in addition to being positive, outgoing, and fun. He later attended USC, became the Treasurer of the State of Arizona, and as of this publication is the Chief Financial Officer of NASA, the National Aeronautics and Space Administration. That's right, we hired the CFO of NASA to babysit our boys...sort of. The point is do what you can to enlist and recruit friends and caregivers who emulate the qualities you want in your children, especially those with influence. Don't leave it up to children themselves, who out of a lack of experience sometimes select fun, outgoing, but character-flawed peers.

The bottom line is the best way to assist a child in identifying a healthy leader is to model one yourself. Most parents base their parenting on what their parents did or did not do. My wife and I had somewhat different parenting approaches because of our personalities and how we were raised.

One of the biggest issues I see among young families today is how they handle screen time. We're tempted to constantly be in front of the television, computer, or phone. A few nights ago my wife and I were eating out, surrounded by four families with children. I noticed that at three of the tables, the parents were each staring at their cell phones, while the kids and in one case, a teen, simply sat and ate their food. I'm amazed at how often I see that. As a parent, think of yourself as the leader of your family organization. Mealtimes should be your staff meetings. Talk to your kids. Set the tone. Make meals a no-screen zone where you focus on face-to-face relationships, not virtual ones.

Leadership is about your ability to connect with people. One of the big challenges organizations face today is young employees who possess technical skills but lack social ones.

Research shows that children under 2 should not have any screen time and kids ages 2 to 4 should be limited to one hour a day. The reason is their brains are still developing significantly, and screen time early on impedes healthy development, not to mention inhibits social skills such as conversation and listening. Please don't do what I see many parents doing, propping up a phone for your child to watch a movie while they interact with others at the table. When you do this, you're missing a great opportunity to model adult conversation and include your child in the world of social interaction.

The fact is, we as parents are the primary influencers in the lives of our kids. How we conduct ourselves at home, respond to conflict, handle disappointments, and our day-to-day attitudes do more to help our children understand what it means to be in community than anything else. Whether or not we're a leader at our work or in our neighborhood, we are seen as leaders in our homes. Think of how you'd like to be led as you lead your family. Then your children will grow up to bless your name, as a proverb says.

The more you can talk about what constitutes a leader, along with qualities that emulate good and bad leading, the more you'll create a mindset for analyzing who they choose to follow and who they choose not to follow. The world doesn't just need better leaders. It also needs smart and savvy followers.

Chapter 28

The 4 Dimensions of Leadership Training

Theme: What young leaders need to know most.

For as long as I can remember, I've been interested in leadership. It began as a child, picking what my friends and I would play at recess in school. This emerged into running for leadership roles in college, starting two organizations from scratch, earning a doctorate in the field, writing a dozen books on the subject, and now teaching leadership and organizational behavior at various universities. I'm not trying to brag. I am trying to explain that I've interacted with scores of leaders in the last 40 years and I've read a lot of the research and thinking about leadership.

One of the great strategies of life is to begin with the end in mind. That's the angle we took when we began looking at how to develop young leaders. While there's very little research specifically on young leader development, there is a lot that deals with what adults seek in their leaders. Therefore, I did an extensive literature review to look at these qualities and then reverse-engineer them, so to speak. If we want to raise leaders who people want to follow, let's focus on these qualities in how we train our children and youth.

If you look at the literature, you'll see an array of themes emerge. Some executive assessments try to measure more than 100 leader qualities. During my studies, I reviewed nearly 700 books and searched thousands of articles related to leadership, leader qualities, and what people liked and disliked about leaders. Because our goal was to simplify, I wanted to see what patterns and categories were the most common.

The end result identified two primary categories, each of which was made up by two subcategories. We refer to these as the four dimensions of leadership training. Then we identified qualities that seemed to fit well into the curriculum. We did not begin with a model and force the literature into it, but rather as we began to see the pattern, we tried to make it balanced and doable as we created our KidLead training curriculum. Hopefully these can help you as an adult as well, but my work and the purpose of this chapter is to offer insights for what you'll want to focus on in developing your child's leadership potential.

The two large categories involve character and competence. At first I was surprised that character-oriented themes were so strong, but when you think about it, a leader's character impacts everyone. It establishes values, ethics, and fairness. What we do and how we do it is often an extension of who we are. Plus a leader's actions and values are amplified, so that a gap in character has far greater negative effect. Within the category of character are two sub-groups: values and attitudes. By values, we mean those that seem most important for leaders to have. When they lack these, everyone suffers. By attitudes, we mean the qualities important to how a leader responds. Awhile back, we talked about the difference between a thermometer and a thermostat. A thermometer tells the temperature, but a thermostat sets the temperature. Since leaders are thermostats, their attitudes are important because they set the tone for the team and organization.

The second large category we mentioned is competence. These involve skills vital for effective leading. There are certain skill sets that separate leaders from others. The two subsets we found in this category are relationships and decisions. By relationships, we mean the ability to understand and get along with people, help them work together, and bring out the best in a team. Leaders are primarily in the people business, helping create synergy so the total output is greater than the sum total of the individual participants. The other subset regarding competence is making decisions.

Leaders must think strategically to make good decisions. People who are not good at making decisions don't become leaders, or they tend not to last long. People need to trust the decision process of those they follow. Without this, they'll be unlikely to commit to goals and projects.

Those are the four dimensions of leadership training, based on an overview of the literature. Now, let me introduce four qualities in each, resulting in a list describing 16 of the most valued characteristics of leaders.

In the dimension of Character Values, people seek these qualities in their leaders: Ethics, Integrity, Responsibility, and Commitment. Ethics pertains to doing the right things, being trustworthy. By integrity we mean being reliable, doing what you say as a leader. It is the glue of trust. Responsibility has to do with dependability, following through with what we begin; and by commitment, we mean persevering, not giving up when things get difficult.

In the dimension of Character Attitudes, people seek these qualities in their leaders: Honor, Confidence, Humility, and Optimism. Honor is the attitude we take toward people, treating them with dignity and respect. By confidence we mean conveying courage and dedication. Humility has to do with leaders being there to serve people, not to be self-centered and self-serving. And optimism is the attitude that fosters hope in others, encouraging them when they get down.

In the dimension of Competence Relationships, people seek these skills in their leaders: Communication, Team, Recruiting, and Conflict Management. Communication is obviously important as leaders must convey information that's understood. By team we mean the importance of helping others work together cohesively. Recruiting has to do with identifying talent and then inviting people to participate in the roles where they'll be successful. And conflict management means keeping the unity, working through differences, and resolving issues that can divide.

In the dimension of Competence Decisions, people seek these skills in their leaders: Power, Vision, Strategy, and Change. Power is understanding influence, where to find it, and how to use it responsibly. Vision is giving people a preferred future, a picture of where they're going and why. Strategy is about developing a plan of how to accomplish goals. And change has to do with making difficult choices for innovation and improvement. These are among the most vital themes regarding a leader's decision making.

You can find more information about this in my book, *The O Factor*. Some of this information is also available on the website, www.KidLead.com.

Let me close this chapter with a little story. A dad was trying to come up with an activity for his child, to preoccupy her for a while so he could finish some work. He removed a page from a magazine that had a picture of the earth and then tore it into pieces. He said, "Here's a puzzle. See if you can put all the pieces together." A few minutes later, his child said, "All done." The dad couldn't believe how fast she'd completed the puzzle. He went into the other room and sure enough, all of the pieces were taped together. "That's amazing. How did you do that so quickly?" he asked. His daughter said, "Easy. On the back was a picture of a person. As soon as I had the person put together, the world was together." The point is that the best way to change the world is to focus on building great people.

As I like to say, "If you want to change the world, focus on leaders. But if you want to change leaders, focus on them when they're young."

Chapter 29

Qualities of a Team

Theme: Explaining how a team operates.

During my organizational behavior and leadership classes that I teach at universities, we talk a lot about teams and how they function. A lot of research has been done to study teams that are effective as opposed to those that are not. I'm almost done writing a book for new managers, titled The Effective Manager. Last month the Gallup organization released a huge study, noting that managers and leaders are the single most important factor in terms of what makes an organization effective. While that may seem like common sense, my point is that there's a lot of research behind this lesson. Helping your young leader understand how teams function is important.

A team is basically defined as two or more people working together to accomplish a common goal. This could be a school assignment, a basketball team, a project group at work, or special ops in the military. Depending on the age of your child, you may need to communicate these ideas in a different manner, but perhaps the easiest is an athletic team. If your child is on a team sport or likes to watch team sports, you can talk about how the team works and how different it would be if a team competed against a single person. For example, what if a basketball team of five people played against a single player? Chances are very high that the team would win.

Teams vary in size, based on the availability of talent and the goal. Ask your child what it would be like if there were 20 people on each team playing on the basketball court. Imagine having 20 people in your house every time you wanted to clean it! Chances are, unless you have a mansion, people would get in the way of each other and it would be chaotic. One thing effective teams have in common is a good leader, someone who helps everyone work together.

Leaders help teams achieve synergy. This is when the output of the team is greater than the sum total of the individuals. A simple thing you can do is get a few beans. Now if your child knows a little bit of math, you can illustrate the power of synergy. Place two beans on the table in front of you on your left and two more beans on your right. Hide two beans in one of your hands. Ask your child to count the beans on the table. She'll say, "Four." Then with your left hand, push two of the beans toward the middle and with your right hand, push the other two beans toward the middle, covering the beans with both hands as you let the two hidden beans come out of your hand. Before you remove your hands, ask your child how many beans there are now. She will say "four." As you remove your hands, you say, "No, it's six!" You can have a little fun with this. It's a simple magic trick illustrating that people accomplish more when they work together than they can when they work alone.

Most teams involve three types of people: a leader, participants, and influencers. In English, this forms an acronym for the word LIP (leader, influencer, participant: L.I.P.). A leader is a person who organizes the team and helps it work together. It may be like a teacher of the class, the coach of a basketball team, or your boss at work. A participant is a person who is a team member. We use the word participant more than follower because a follower is more passive, but an active team member participates. It's the difference between a basketball player who is sitting on the bench, ready to go into the game, versus a spectator in the stand who is merely watching. The fan isn't on the team.

We also teach about a third member on most teams. We refer to this person as an influencer. An influencer is a participant who tends to get others to do things the leader wants or doesn't want. This person isn't the official leader and may not even want to lead or know how to lead, but the influencer still makes people think and act differently. It is important for a team leader to know who the influencers are so that he can get the influencer on his side. If he doesn't do that, the influencer may work against the leader and the team won't be united.

Whenever I teach on teams in the university, I discuss the importance of determining when a team is needed and when it isn't. Sometimes, because teams are so popular now in business, we start thinking everything should be done as a team—but this isn't true. Sometimes individuals are more productive when working alone. Again, you'll need to come up with some examples that your child will understand. A simple one might be cleaning your child's bedroom. It may be easier to do it herself because she knows how she wants her room to look. Plus getting everyone together at the same time might be difficult. Doing it alone, she can do it whenever she wants. Also, it might be difficult with a bunch of people in a small room. Working alone, she wouldn't have to settle arguments or clean up after them when they put her toys or clothes where they didn't belong. Smart leaders know when to work as a team and when to let people work alone.

Let's end this chapter with an activity you can do to discuss the differences between working as a team and working alone. You'll need three or four people and a box of 100 paper clips. You'll do three rounds of this activity. The goal is to make the longest paper-clip chain you can in 30 seconds, so obviously you'll need a timer as well. A chain means you'll link the paper clips end to end. You can't use any clips that are already connected, only single ones. During the first round, each person will work alone. Then count each chain. Most people get 6-12. But in the second round, you'll work together as a team to create a chain. Again, you can only use individual clips, so you may need to take some apart.

Take a minute to strategize before you start. Let your child lead the team. Then make the chain. Count how many are in it. Most times you'll have 20-30. Occasionally the total goes down because the team ran into a problem. That's okay. Do a third round as a team again. Like before, you'll have 30 seconds and you can only use individual clips. Take a minute to strategize. After time is up, count how many were in the chain. Chances are you'll see a big improvement. Then compare the differences between the third round team chain and the first round individual chain. Ask questions such as what made the difference, why do teams often outperform individuals, and what makes organizing a team difficult?

Activities like these, whether it's cleaning up after a meal together, putting away groceries after a shopping trip, or packing for a vacation offer opportunities to discuss the strengths of teams as well as how they operate. Helping young leaders think about performance, accomplishment, and running a team are important to creating a leadership mindset. Eventually, your young leader will be leading teams at home, school, and the neighborhood, all great practice for leading effectively as an adult.

Chapter 30

Recruiting a Strong Team

Theme: Teaching young leaders about what it means to put together a good team.

When I was a child, I remember playing Red Rover, Red Rover. It's a game where two teams of kids form a line facing each other, 30-40 feet apart. One team holds hands to form a human fence. Then they select a person from the other team and chant, "Red Rover, Red Rover, send Jonathan right over." Jonathan then runs toward the other team and tries to break through the hands of two people. If he can't break the chain, Jonathan stays and joins that team. If he gets through, he picks someone from that team to go to his side. The goal is to get all of the other team members to your team.

The game starts with two team captains. They face everyone else who is standing in a long row. The captains take turns, one by one, selecting people from the line who then get behind the leader. The captains want the strongest kids and those who are really good at holding on, so their team's chain will be strong. Usually the smallest kids get picked last because they're the least likely to help the team succeed.

No one likes being picked last. I'm not necessarily an advocate of putting kids into situations where they are picked last or made to feel inferior. Yet this is an illustration of how life works. Organizations, small and large, seek individuals who will perform well. We've all worked with people who just didn't seem to fit. Either they didn't have the right education or skill or experience, or perhaps they were lazy or difficult to work with because of their personality. That's why getting the right people on the bus is such an important leadership ability.

The first step in recruiting a strong team is identifying the tasks required to achieve what the team needs to accomplish. A computer company would have different roles than a restaurant, school, or manufacturing company. So before a leader thinks of people, she needs to consider the tasks to be accomplished and then what skills are needed to do these tasks.

Here are some ways to help your child begin thinking this way. Start with everyday experiences. For example, if you're in a restaurant, a conversation could go something like this:

"Josh, what do you think it takes to make this restaurant operate?"

"What do you mean?" your child asks.

"I mean, who are the different people on staff and what do they do?"

Josh looks around, "Well, you need servers, people who ask what you want and then bring your food."

"Good, that's right," you say. "Who else?"

"You need cooks to make the food."

"That's right. Keep going, who else?"

Josh ponders a bit, then says, "The lady when we came in, who showed us what table to sit at."

"Yes, the hostess. Anyone else?"

Josh sees a man removing dirty dishes and cleaning the tables. "That guy over there is cleaning the tables."

"That's a busboy, good. Can you think of anyone else?"

Josh pauses and then says "No."

You continue, "What about the person who washes the dishes, along with the pots and pans that get dirty by the cooks? Just like at home, someone would need to wash them." Josh nods. Then you add, "There would need to be someone who oversees everything, making sure the right people were scheduled and that they had enough to serve the customers. This might be a manager or the owner of the restaurant. Then someone else would need to pay the bills, count the money, and make sure people got paid, like a bookkeeper." This kind of conversation goes on so that Josh begins to see the various roles and how many tasks need to be completed.

You can do this in any number of settings, whether you're shopping in a store, watching television, discussing your child's school, or as you discuss athletic teams. The next step is to figure out qualities and skills needed to complete the tasks. In the restaurant example, you can ask your child what is required to succeed in a role. For example, the cook should know how to use recipes, to make the food taste good. The cashier should be good with money. The hostess should be friendly and polite. The food servers should be able to carry the heavy trays and be friendly as well.

Naturally, these skills differ from organization to organization and from role to role. The goal is to think about the kind of talent each role needs.

Next, help your child analyze the qualities of the people they see. For example, you might say, "What were some of the good qualities of the hostess?" Josh says, "She smiled and was polite and handed us a menu." "That's right," you say. "Do you think there was anything she might do better next time?" Josh thinks a bit and says, "Maybe she could have asked me at the start if I wanted the coloring page, instead of us having to ask for it later." "Good, good," you say. "How do you think her boss could train her to do that?" "Well, maybe he could remind her that when kids come in the door, automatically ask them if they want the coloring page."

As your child develops his or her leadership potential, you can get into more sophisticated discussions such as how to motivate and develop team members, or even the need from time to time to un-invite people from a team, often known as letting someone go or firing someone. Because most adults do this poorly, how wonderful it would be if leaders learned how to graciously let people go or move them to other roles with dignity. You can even discuss your experiences in this area.

The goal is to develop a child who sees what others his age do not, to be aware of what it takes to run a team, along with the tasks and skills and talent needed to accomplish them. Creating an organizational mindset is important for developing leadership skills, because leaders need to recruit the right people. This is one of the most difficult things leaders do. Effective ones are good at putting together strong teams and inviting talented people to be on the team. As your child develops a basic understanding of tasks needed and skills required, you can begin talking about how to ask and persuade others to be on their team. The most natural places for this are on athletic teams, school assignments, and home projects that you design for your child to lead.

By starting young to help your child see what it takes to succeed as a team, you'll be developing some of the most important skills required for leading.

Chapter 31

Effective Communication Skills

Theme: Training young leaders to have effective communication skills.

Every year, organizational research includes what companies look for most in new employees. Consistently, at or near the top of the list is the ability to communicate well. For years, I've taught writing and speaking skills to university students. My graduate degree is in communication psychology. My studies in leadership reveal that the ability to communicate is an essential for leaders. I've written 25 books and hundreds of articles and made over 2000 speeches in addition to my lectures as a professor, so I don't just teach communication, I also live it. I'm continually striving to improve my craft. The good news is that you can give your child a head start in this area, so whether or not your child has leadership talent, you can help him or her develop strong communication skills.

Why is communication so important to leading? A leader needs to be able to convey her ideas to others so they understand what she means. Whether it's vision casting, inspiring, explaining problems and solutions, or even facilitating meetings, communication is key to effective leading. You can communicate without leading, but you can't lead well without communicating effectively. Right or wrong, people judge you on your ability to communicate. If you do it poorly, they won't respect your intellect or ideas. If you do it well, people place more value on them than they should.

Communication is also important for leaders because they're frequently asked to make speeches and lead meetings. They're a spokesperson for their team and company. My home is only a 7-minute drive to the Ronald Reagan Presidential Library. The only non-family member photo I have in my office is that of President Reagan. He is my favorite modern U.S. President, and he is referred to as the "great communicator" because of his ability to engage audiences, inspire people, and make complicated issues understandable.

In this chapter I'm going to focus only on verbal communication, not writing. You can divide oral communication into two categories: formal and informal. By formal we mean making speeches in front of others where everyone is focused on you. By informal, we're referring to small group facilitation, one-on-one, and interpersonal communication. Let me give you a few of the things we strive to accomplish in our KidLead training.

In formal communication, focus on the following three things. The first is nonverbal, the second is opening and closing, and the third is path. By nonverbal, we mean things like poise, gestures, smiling, projection, and eye contact. Depending on the study you read, 30-70% of communication impact is nonverbal, meaning how you say something can be more important than what you say. Help your child smile and make eye contact with the audience. This conveys warmth, confidence, and trust. Video record your child making 1- to 3-minute speeches so she can see what she looks like. Help her focus on standing erect, not leaning or swaying. Encourage her to use her hands and look at her entire audience, not just straight ahead.

In our KidLead training curriculum, many of our mini-projects include a presentation portion at the end. This gives participants an opportunity to stand in front of their peers and practice speaking. The more you can do this, the more familiar a child becomes with speaking, resulting in more confident and competent communicators. Come up with weekly speeches where your child presents his highlights of the week or shares a report done in school.

In addition, introduce your child to great orators. Many great speakers can be seen on the internet. Don't just listen to the content; look at the nonverbal parts, how he gestures, moves, smiles, and looks at his audience. Point these out to your child.

A second issue to teach your child about is the opening and closing of a speech. These are the two most important times. You only have about 20 seconds to grab someone's attention. In a busy world, people automatically ask themselves, "Why should I listen to you?" This relates to primacy and recency. Primacy refers to first impressions. As the saying goes, "You only have one chance to make a good first impression." Recency refers to the last thing said. The first and last are remembered the longest, so start with your second best point and end with the best. It may involve starting with a joke, an attention-getting story, or a provocative question. The ending should involve a call to action, what you want the audience to do, or a story to grab their emotions so they remember the speaker.

The third issue is path, referring to how the content is organized. Speeches should lead somewhere. What's the path? If you don't provide clear structure, you'll lose your listeners between the start and finish. Providing direction and a logical progression are important speech issues. Work with your child in outlining the speech and thinking it through.

Now let's discuss informal communication. These are situations where a person is in charge, but not necessarily on a stage or behind a podium. One way to practice facilitating a meeting is when you're eating a meal together. Ask your child to periodically lead dinner conversations. Put the cell phones away. Meals should be a no-screens zone. You might say, "Keri, tonight is your turn to lead our family discussion. You can ask us how our days went, what we did, and maybe share one high and one low, meaning a happy experience and a sad one. You can ask us questions and help us stay on task. How does that sound to you?" "Great," your daughter says.

When you think about it, most family mealtimes have a lot of similarities to company meetings, even if they're not as agenda driven. You still have an agenda, such as finding out how everyone's day went, reporting on experiences, and discussing plans for the next few days. By frequently delegating leadership to your child and offering coaching cues, the more comfortable your child will become facilitating group discussions.

Remember to emphasize listening skills, eye contact, smiling, affirmation, and keeping the group on topic. These are all relevant skills for leading any team, and they focus on communication. You can actually create a simple score card, offering rewards to your child when they do these well. Video tape your family meetings, offering affirmations along with suggestions of how to be even better next time.

One more thing: practicing meeting new people. I realize there may be cultural issues here, but teach your child customary gestures such as shaking hands, looking people in the eyes, and smiling when being introduced to them. This might be another adult, a boss, or a peer. A child's ability to do these things makes a strong first impression that lingers in the mind of others. The new person will think, "Wow, this young person is confident and very adult-like." It's a great way to convey leadership potential. Children who do not look adults in the eyes or extend a hand or stand erect when meeting a peer or adult communicate insecurity, immaturity, and intimidation. Practice these skills at home, then with your extended family, and then with people in your network. Most parents don't include their children in introductions like these, but they miss great opportunities for training. As you do this, you'll see significant improvements. Your child will distinguish himself from other kids his age.

Communicating well is a great asset for everyone, but it's essential for leaders. Start this early and your child will excel.

Chapter 32

Managing Conflict

Theme: Training young leader how to handle disagreements.

In this chapter, we're going to talk about how to teach your child to manage conflict.

I am an only child, so whenever I had a conflict with my parents, I lost. Although I love my parents, I didn't grow up seeing conflict resolved well. Too often there was yelling and unhealthy anger. Raising three sons out own, I see so many opportunities I missed to learn how to resolve conflict with peers early in life. My wife was exceptionally good at managing conflict, so I've learned a lot watching her. Now I teach conflict management to business school students, discussing the research behind this field, as well as offering practical tools that leaders can use to handle it effectively.

Someone said, "If you can't stand the heat, get out of the kitchen." I like a variation of that for leaders which is, "If you can't create some heat, get out of the kitchen." Leaders must learn how to manage conflict well because they frequently find themselves in situations where they create conflict by decisions they make, innovating new practices and ideas, and of course resolving issues among team members. The natural approach to managing conflict is to suppress it. But this isn't good for families or for organizations.

There are two kinds of conflict: functional and dysfunctional. Functional conflict focuses on issues and allows people to convey their differing opinions so that those involved learn from it and often result in better outcomes. Good companies benefit from functional conflict and sometimes even create it, because a lack of conflict can be unhealthy. Most of us are more familiar with dysfunctional conflict, the kind that focuses on people and ruins relationships. The best thing you can do as a parent to instill strong conflict management skills in your kids is to model the way you resolve conflict in your family. Here are five conflict management skills that we teach young leaders. Each one is designed to result in unifying a team and avoid dysfunctional conflict that injures unity. Each is effective when used in the right situation, but each style also has weaknesses. Therefore, the key is to use the appropriate style for the situation, much like having a toolbox. You don't use a hammer to put a nut on a bolt. Nor do you use a screwdriver to drive a nail. Selecting the right tool for the job is the key to conflict management as well.

The first conflict management style is collaboration, also known as problem solving. Every conflict should start with this approach, because the goal is to identify the problem and then solve it. The focus here is the problem, not the person. Even if one child hits another, the problem is the behavior, not the person. It could focus on constructive ways to respond to anger, to use words before actions, and understanding how to communicate wants. See it as a game to play, a mystery to solve, a goal to achieve. Because it's often difficult to know which conflict management style to apply immediately, the collaboration style is the best one to begin with.

For example, let's say your child and a friend are in a conflict over some toy building blocks. A quick conversation might go like this.

"Jonathan, I can tell that you're angry. It's okay to be angry. I get angry at times. What's making you feel mad?"

He says, "Susie is playing with my blocks and I asked her not to because I don't want her to mess up my building."

You say, "Good. Susie, why do you think it's okay to play with the blocks in Jonathan's building?"

She says, "Because he wasn't playing with them anymore and I wanted to use them. He can make the building over again when I'm done."

You respond, "Good. I can understand both of your points. So what would be a way to resolve this problem?"

That kind of conversation is problem-solution oriented. It may end up with something as simple as leaving the blocks in the building, with Susie using those not in the building. There may be other ideas, but if not, the conflict management style may need to incorporate one of the other four that I'll introduce now.

A second conflict management style is compromising. This is a strong style when those involved in the conflict can't seem to resolve the issue through collaboration. Plus collaboration takes more time, so if you don't have time, getting each side to give up something and meet in the middle may be the best. The downside of compromising is that sometimes your best decisions come by working through them, so that you don't have to give up as much.

A third conflict management style is directive. This approach is more competitive in nature and strong handed. Even though using it too much is destructive, resulting in people disliking you and creating division on a team, it is useful when you need people to resolve an issue in a crisis and when you have a strong personality on the team who will intimidate others if given an opportunity. In the right situation, being bold and direct is what is needed. Use it too much and you'll come across as bossy, disrespectful, and people will resent you.

A fourth conflict management style is accommodating. This is where one party gives in to the other party's wish. This is helpful when retaining peace is important. It can be powerful when saving the relationship is more important than the issue. It's also a tool to help the person giving in get what he or she wants later. "I'll give you what you want now, because I may need you to give me what I want later." It's called *quid pro quo*, this for that. "I'll scratch your back. You scratch mine." The weakness of this style is that if one person does more accommodating, the other will start taking advantage and begin assuming that he or she will always get their way. This creates a lopsided relationship that is unhealthy and can result in dysfunctional conflict.

A fifth conflict management style is avoiding. This is where one or more people in the conflict simply ignore it. This can be good when someone needs time to cool off, to get into an emotional state that is more controlled and positive. Avoiding is also good when you need time to do more research, to get more facts for better understanding. The weakness of avoiding is that ignoring a problem can make it worse, like not treating a cut or a splinter in a finger. Infection can set in and people get sick. Plus leaders can lose the respect of their followers.

Hopefully as a parent you can come up with ways to convey these styles that are appropriate to your child's age and social-emotional maturity level. The point is to teach these styles so that when conflict occurs, you can offer coaching to discuss effective ways of dealing with conflicts, to keep them functional and not dysfunctional. My wife and I tried to keep the rules of our family simple. They were: "We don't hurt people and we don't hurt things and we don't hurt ourselves." We chanted that motto time after time, helping our sons remember them when needed.

Allowing children to work through their conflict is important, even if it is not pleasant. Giving them tools and teaching them how to use them will give them power in relationships. Dysfunctional conflict hurts people, so learning how to manage it well is a lifelong skill, important for everyone, but essential for leading.

Chapter 33

Tapping Power Sources

Theme: Understanding and tapping six sources of power.

One of the most important topics in organizational behavior and leadership is power and influence. The reason it is so important is that power is needed to lead. A powerless leader is an oxymoron; it doesn't exist. When you cease to have power, you can no longer lead others. Power is neither good nor bad. How you use it determines whether it is good or bad.

One of the best ways to teach this to a child is using the example of electricity. No doubt you've taught your child, at a very young age, not to place his fingers into the electrical outlets in your home. That is because touching electricity will harm us. Electricity, if not used properly, can also start fires. When wiring is bad, it can also ruin machines and equipment. But the same electricity can cook our food, light our house, and keep us safe and alive. The power of electricity is not good or bad; it's how it is used. Yet it's very important. As we've mentioned before, this will typically be more difficult for children under 10 to understand, because power and influence are concepts. We'll offer more tangible teaching ideas in this chapter.

In organizational behavior and leadership, *power is typically defined as the potential to influence, and influence is defined as power activated.* Although this is a somewhat complex topic, it's an important one to explain to young leaders because when you're young, you rarely have legitimate authority that comes with holding a position, such as a teacher, principal, manager, or CEO. We touched on this topic in another chapter, discussing leading up, referring to tapping other people's influence, but our focus today is broader.

Emerging leaders often think that they can't lead until they become an adult and get appointed to an official position. But positional leadership is actually only one of seven power resources. We're going to explain the six legitimate sources so that hopefully you can teach these to your child at his or her level of maturity.

Let's start with the power resource that is the most obvious, **position and authority**. Influence that comes from this power resource relates to a person's role and title in an organization. This is the easiest one to teach to children, because they understand the position of a teacher, your role as a parent, and the authority of a police officer. While we want to teach respect for people in positions, we also know that throughout history, those who used their positions for evil, to hurt people, sometimes needed to be removed from these positions. There are many children's stories about evil rulers, kings, and queens. Until a young leader has a formal position, she will need to lead up or resort to the other five sources as follows.

A second power source is officially called **referent**, but it refers to people and relationships. This also ties into the idea of leading up, but it goes beyond that. This is not about what you know but who you know. Many people have power because they know a lot of people and/or they have relationships with people who possess things that are valuable to them.

One way to teach this concept to your child is thinking of how other people can help him. For example, you might ask your child to list five or six people he knows personally, and then list at least one way that person can help him. For example, a teacher could give him valuable knowledge. A coach could show him a new skill. As a parent, you can provide food and a place to live. A friend can help him have fun when playing. Each of the people in his network brings a value. Therefore, this power source involves expanding one's network and also getting to know people who can help in different areas.

A third source of power that leaders can use is **information and knowledge**. This is why people invest in quality education, because knowledge is power. The ability to access information is also valuable and a source of power. When you are limited in your ability to acquire knowledge, it is a reduction in power and access to influence. A way to explain this power source to your child is talking about school and then asking them questions, such as math or another topic that they can answer now but could not at a younger age before they'd learned it in school. It could also be as simple as having the combination to unlock a padlock or a password to a cell phone or laptop. Info and knowledge are strong ways to acquire power.

A fourth source of power for leaders is **talent and expertise**. This is more about what you can do better than others. Expertise is a skill gained through experience and familiarity. Talent is having a special ability that is desirable in an organization. For example, a person with coding skills would be more valuable to a computer software company than an agriculture corporation. People with stronger talent and expertise are in greater demand, giving them more power and influence, usually resulting in higher pay. This is a relatively easy source to teach your children, as you can relate it to sports, movies, or other areas where talent determines who has greater influence.

A fifth source for obtaining power is **resources**. We talked about position, but this is about possession, what you own. Examples of resource influence are money, physical and military strength, land, stocks in a wealthy company, and any number of physical items. This is why strong countries maintain large militaries, to retain power and, if needed, influence. Money is the obvious item in this category because it can obtain many other resources. But one item often overlooked is time. Although time is not tangible, it can be powerful. As the saying goes, time is money. A way to teach this to your child could be money, having the power to buy an item he wants. You could also arm wrestle your child, illustrating physical strength.

A sixth source of power is **personality and charisma**. Some people are more likable and persuasive, simply because of their temperament and how they come across to others. Naturally, you can see how some of these sources interact with each other. For example, a person who is outgoing and charismatic is probably going to have a larger network, and therefore also possess referent power. That is why teaching your child good communication skills, how to start a conversation with someone, make eye contact and offer firm handshakes are all vital for this. Children who are more introverted and intimidated limit their power. You can practice these with your child, as we discussed in the chapter on communication skills.

I mentioned there are seven primary sources of power, but only six legitimate ones. So in closing, let me tell you about the seventh power source. It is **coercion and fear**. We talked about this in another chapter, when we discussed identifying and standing up to bullies. When a person or organization changes the behavior of people through force and fear, it is rarely good. It's a negative use of power because it dishonors people and nearly always leads to a revolt. That is why we want to teach young leaders how to gain power and use it well, so they can help people and stand up to those who use power to harm others. Power and influence are the currency of leadership.

Chapter 34

Vision

Theme: How to help children understand vision.

Ironically (or not), I'm writing this chapter on the 50th anniversary of humans first landing on the moon. I remember as a child, in 1969, watching an astronaut named Neil Armstrong on a black and white television. I, along with 650 million others, heard him say, "That's one small step for man. One giant leap for mankind." And now, 50 years later, the U.S. is revisiting plans to develop projects on the moon.

But several years before humans landed on the moon, President John F. Kennedy made a bold vision cast. In 1961, he said that by the end of the decade, we will land a man on the moon. This vision created both a destination to reach and a motivation to get there. It was known as his moonshot speech. When I was introducing KidLead to China, I had the opportunity to speak at Moonshot Academy in Beijing, a school named after the idea of following a vision and creating visionary leaders.

Of all the important leadership principles, vision may be the most difficult to teach and learn. Thus, it's often considered one of those things that you either have or you don't. You can't be a great leader if you don't know how to cast a compelling vision. So while it comes naturally to transformational leaders, I think it is possible to teach skills that lend themselves to vision casting.

First, what is a vision? A vision is different from a dream, a plan, a goal, or a mission. Dreams tend to be personal and somewhat difficult to define. A vision is more corporate in nature, engaging others to get involved and work together. A vision statement tends to have more specifics. In Martin Luther King Junior's famous "I have a dream speech," he provided examples of what life in America would be like when all ethnicities had equality. It's a preferred future, a place we want to go, as in President Kennedy's moonshot speech. At the same time, a vision lacks clarity on how it is going to be accomplished. Those are the things that plans and goals involve. Goals often aren't necessarily inspiring and can be somewhat sterile of emotion, but visions compel us. They make us want to jump on and follow, or they at least make us want to watch.

A vision statement is different from a mission. Most companies today have some sort of mission, describing what they do and why they do it. This helps guide how the organization functions and why it is in existence. A vision is different because it is more specific. While grounded in the mission, it is a declaration of what's ahead, with sufficient details to recognize it once we arrive.

A quality vision can be judged on three components: size, specificity, and brevity. If it's not going to stretch us, it probably won't inspire people to greatness, and it's likely more of a goal in nature. If it lacks specificity, it will be unclear in the minds of people and is more of a dream or general inclination. Finally, a strong vision is brief. It needs to be easily repeatable, much like President Kennedy's bold declaration of landing a man on the moon before the end of the decade. Some of the greatest speeches throughout history have been very short. If it takes too much explaining to be understood, it is less apt to make a significant impact.

Another way of understanding a vision is that it describes a reality that has not yet happened. This reality is nearly always beyond what seems normal or natural, certainly not status quo. A vision stretches us. Great inventors were nearly always visionary. Henry Ford believed that every family could own a gas engine car. The Wright Brothers were convinced people could fly. Steve Jobs visualized everyday folk owning computers that were easy to use and intuitive. Naturally, all visions don't become reality, but those that do are transformational.

Although vision is one of the 16 characteristics in our LeadYoung Training curricula, it is the single most challenging one to teach. But here are some ideas that I think can help you as a parent develop your child's vision casting potential.

First, fan the flames of your child's imagination. Studies show the rapid decline of creativity in children as they age. Some blame it on the format of modern education, where a teacher stands in front of a class teaching them what and how to think. They don't reward coloring outside the lines, as we say. Conformity, compliance, and consistency tend to dissolve the ability to think creatively. While they're young, most children are naturally creative, so do what you can to affirm this. Celebrate creative activities and accomplishments. Play make believe with your child, even if you're a more serious person by nature.

If possible, enroll your child into programs that lend themselves to creativity. A big thing is schooling. My wife home schooled our sons for several years. That's one idea. Our oldest son and his wife have their daughters enrolled in a Montessori-type school, where the pedagogy is more experiential and less about rote learning. If this isn't feasible for you, then enroll them in after school programs where creativity is fostered, such as art, dance, acting, robotics, and entrepreneurism.

A second thing you can do is introduce them to visionary leaders. Listening to inspiring speakers, big thinking people who challenge us to look differently at ourselves and what we can achieve, reflect vision

DNA. Look for visionary movies and even television shows where one of the characters gets his or her friends together to do something bold and exciting. Talk about this afterward so that your child can learn to distinguish what a vision is from other speeches and talks. Look for opportunities to hear visionary speakers, but also be sure to explain what it is. Look for the three components we discussed earlier.

A third thing you can do is to begin encouraging vision casting around your home. I know this may sound a little funny, but hang in there a second while I describe it. Help your child come up with declarations related to a preferred future. This may have to do with a school event, a big athletic game, or even a family outing such as a weekend trip or vacation. For example, a declarative statement about a preferred future could be something such as, "We are going to have a truly amazing day at the zoo!" or even "This year we are going to take the best family vacation we've ever had." You can even make it a contest to come up with vision statements like these. There will be some laughter and silliness, but it's about creating excitement for a future reality.

Naturally, casting a vision is more than merely stating a single sentence about what you hope for in the future, but it does offer a start for what may be the most difficult thing to teach and the single most unique thing that leaders do differently from others. Getting people excited about an idea of a preferred future reality is the essence of vision casting. Assisting your child in developing this skill can help him or her get a big head start on leading.

Chapter 35

Thinking Strategically

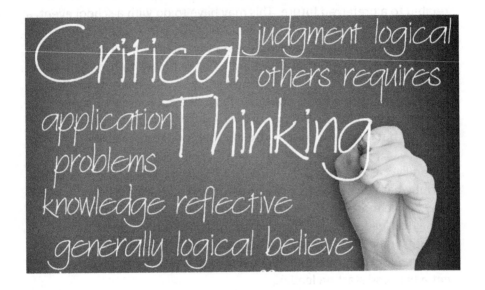

Theme: Ideas to help young leaders develop strategic thinking.

One of the highlights of my life involved getting an insider's tour of the NASA Mission Control Center in Houston, Texas. Some of my students at the time were NASA engineers, so they got me into some behind-the-scenes opportunities. One of these included getting to sit in the chair of Gene Krantz, the flight director who oversaw mission control during the Apollo 11 mission, where man first walked on the moon. He also supervised the Apollo 13 mission, where a fire broke out and the team on the ground had to come up with a strategic way to save the astronauts and bring them safely back to earth. It's the famous scene when the astronaut says, "Houston, we have a problem."

That's what effective leaders are good at, helping their teams come up with solutions to problems. The problem might be fixing a piece of equipment or achieving a goal. It's a matter of getting from Point A, where we are, to Point B, where we want to be. To get from A to B requires a strategy. Leaders help their teams strategize. The idea of teaching a young leader, especially a child, how to think strategically may seem far-fetched, but actually it's not. In fact, most children naturally do it without thinking about it, but we want them to do it more intentionally. Here are some ideas on how to do that.

A good strategy, in the context of leading, will usually have three ingredients. First, there's a goal. As we said, that goal could be a problem to solve or something to achieve. Second, there's a team. Leaders are social architects, so if you're doing this alone, it doesn't require leadership. And third, it results in a plan of how to get from point A to point B. Therefore, if you want to help your child learn strategy in the context of leading, you'll need to make sure these three ingredients are available. Think of them with three words: what, who, how. What do we want to accomplish? Who is participating? and How are we going to do it?

One way to illustrate this is to show your child a map. If possible, print a street map with your home address and then a site that is some distance from it, at least 2 to 5 miles away. This could be a school, park, or shopping mall. Then, with some markers, ask your child to come up with the three best ways to get from your house to the site. This represents the goal, getting from point A to point B. The paths are potential strategies, resulting in the plan of the preferred route. Then take out your smartphone to find out what your GPS app recommends is the best route, based on time. Compare this with the paths selected on the map. Discuss the differences and perhaps why some might be shorter yet take more time, or longer but be faster. This illustrates a way that your child can see you strategize every day, without thinking much about it.

This automatically employs skills we've discussed in another chapter, related to problem solving and critical thinking. These are a significant part of how leaders strategize with a team. The goal is to come up with multiple paths and then consider which ones are most effective and why. The process itself helps the brain exercise strategic thinking.

Because humans are goal-striving beings, they're drawn to solving puzzles and figuring out problems. But like humans, sometimes we get lazy and don't think hard enough about finding the best way. That's why the saying goes, "The enemy of great is good." We settle for a good strategy instead of pursuing a great one.

Here's an idea you can use that illustrates any number of project-based, active-learning lessons. This one is taken right out of our KidLead training curriculum, where we teach children, preteens, and teens how to lead. All you need for this activity is a stack of about 100 index cards and a measuring tape.

The goal of this project is to build a tower as tall as possible within five minutes. This can happen on the floor or table, but it must be freestanding, so no use of tape or fasteners, and it can't lean on anything. Plus, it must be at least 1 meter in height. Hopefully you'll have three or four people available so that it's truly a team project, and you'll designate your child as the team leader. If you have more, you can have multiple teams and create a competition.

You can say, "Let's build a tower. We have this stack of cards, and our goal is to build the tallest freestanding tower we can with it in five minutes, but it must be at least 1 meter tall. Sonya, you'll be the team leader, so your job is to help us figure out how we should do this." Obviously, depending on Sonya's age and leadership talent, you may need to offer various coaching questions. Don't tell her what to do, but rather ask questions such as, "How do you think you can develop ideas from your team?" "What are three ways we could accomplish this?" and "What tasks do you want to assign each person?"

This is the strategizing portion of the process, where Sonya helps the team brainstorm ideas. As a coach you might want to help this process, because what usually happens is children and preteens jump on the first good idea instead of considering the best idea from multiple ones. The cards must remain in a single stack. They can't be prepared ahead of time. After two to three minutes of strategizing, say "Go" and start the time. Offer 2-minute and 1-minute warnings, and then say "Stop." Measure the tower and state its height.

Then announce there will be a second round. The goal this time is to build the tower taller than the first. Sonya will have another two to three minutes to re-strategize with the team, since now they will have a better understanding of how to improve. The cards must be restacked into a single deck. Sometimes, improvements have to do with how the cards are folded or who is going to do what differently. After the strategizing, say "Go" and start the clock. Offer 2-minute and 1-minute warnings, and then say "Stop." Measure the tower and state its height. See if it is taller than the first round.

Then announce that you're going to have a third round. The goal of this round is to build the tallest tower yet. As before, take time for Sonya to re-strategize with her team, as they make sure all of the cards are restacked into a single pile. Run the time as before, and then measure to see how the team did.

Afterward, do a debrief to discuss how the team developed ideas, the role of the leader in helping the team strategize, what they learned from each round, and what they continued to do the same and what they changed. Project-based activities like these are fun, but they also teach fundamentals in both leading and strategic thinking. You can create any number of mini-projects like these that intentionally focus on What, Who, and How, resulting in a plan.

Eventually, as your young leader's experience grows and she or he develops, you can have them lead more complex projects, strategizing things such as group school assignments, family outings, and even community events. Feel free to share your own experiences with work projects. Don't just talk about the successes. Describe the failures. We often learn more from these, so explain what was learned and how you'd do things differently. This is what we refer to as a postmortem, analyzing what might improve the outcomes next time. Feel free to use the terms such as brainstorming, strategizing, and planning. These are all the vocabulary that leaders use as they help people accomplish goals together.

Chapter 36

Handling Change

Theme: Ideas to help young leaders become agents of change.

One of my favorite subjects is organizational change. The reason, I assume, is that change is at the heart of leading. If you want to be a leader, you have to be willing to catalyze change. If you can't initiate and manage change, then you won't ever be a strong leader. So while change is one of the more sophisticated topics to train young leaders on, it's one of the 16 qualities included in our KidLead curriculum because it's that essential to leading.

When our three sons were very young, one of them got his fingers shut in a car door. I don't recall the details, but obviously it was an accident. We were quite upset. We took our son to the doctor, and he gave us a sense of peace because he said children's bones are very flexible and not yet hardened. Therefore, it's rare for children to break bones like fingers. As we grow older, our bones become more brittle. My wife leads a senior living center. A fall by a senior adult often results in broken bones because theirs are not flexible. The same is true emotionally. People tend to become less and less amenable to change as they age. Children and youth are far more emotionally agile.

John Kotter, a professor at Harvard, noted that 70% of all organizational change projects fail. William Bridges, in his book *Managing the Transitions*, denotes the difference between an innovation plan and a transition plan. The former is about what you want to change, but the latter refers to how you're going to do it. He says that most change efforts fail because we focus on the what and not the how. Bridges goes on to say that change is the physical difference, while a transition is the emotional process.

A good teacher understands his or her students. Therefore, one of the things you can do to determine how accepting or resistant your child will be to change is to figure out his or her wiring.

In his book *The Diffusion of Innovation*, Everett Rogers denotes different kinds of personalities and how they respond to change. In a normal bell-shaped curve, only 15% of people are creative or progressive, meaning they readily embrace and enjoy change. About 35% of people are the early majority, meaning they accept an innovation after the more progressive people have demonstrated that it's viable and beneficial. The later majority, equivalent to 35% of people, will adopt a new idea only once it has been accepted by most of the early majority. They don't trust the creative and progressive minority. Finally, on the tail end of the curve are the laggards. This 15 percent accept new ideas kicking and screaming. They're not bad people. They just don't like the unfamiliar. Their negativity usually is just fear of the unknown.

The first question you need to answer, before you try to teach your child about change, is which of the four groups he or she is in. Children who are on the left side of the curve are far more open to new experiences than others. They're also more likely to be wired to lead, because leaders tend to be less change-aversive. Following are a couple of ideas that you can use if your child is more open to change, because they're more apt to benefit from the training and less likely to respond negatively to it.

Here's a fun activity you can do with your child to teach the concept of change. It's similar to a mini-project in our KidLead training curriculum. Get a variety of clothes, such as two or three shirts, hats, shorts, socks, and shoes. Then, write the name of a clothing item in the pile on a slip of paper, one per slip. You'll place these in a paper bag or bowl. Place the items at the end of a room and then put the bowl at the other end. Get in a line behind the bowl. The first person picks a slip of paper, reads it, runs to the other end of the room to put on the item on the slip of paper, and then runs back to the bowl. Then the next person takes a slip of paper, runs to the clothing pile, and puts on the clothing item. Keep doing this, but each time the person draws a new piece of paper, she or he takes off the first clothing item and places it back on the pile.

After you've done this a number of times, talk about what it felt like to change clothes so quickly. What made it fun? What made it difficult? How is this like making other types of changes in life, such as a new school, new home, new class, and new friends? This is an opportunity to talk about the challenges of adjusting to new things.

Another idea to help your child experience change is to rearrange your child's room when he or she is at school. You can put the bed at a different angle or move it to another side of the room. Move the dresser, change the drawers in the dresser, and reorganize the closet. You can rehang pictures and do a variety of changes. When your child comes home, observe her response. Have some fun with it. Then talk to her about how she felt about the changes. What is it like when others make changes without our permission? Why should we explain changes to people before we do them? What are examples of changes in your life? Did you like them or not? Obviously, out of respect for your child, you can work together to return things as they were, but it will certainly be an experience long remembered.

Here's one more activity that you can do, allowing your child to lead a change experience for everyone else. You'll need three or four people to participate. Get four or five table games or games that your child likes to play. Bring them together in a central location. The objective of this activity is to play a single game for 10 minutes. Then your child will select a different game. She or he will explain instructions. This goes on for 30-60 minutes, each time allowing the young leader to determine what game is being played and making sure that everyone understands how to play it.

After the allotted time, remember to discuss the experience. The goal is not just to have a fun activity, but to also create an environment where your young leader has experience leading change. You can talk about the challenge of getting people's attention, handling disappointment when moving from a game that was enjoyable, and the difficulty of communicating instructions for a new game that others may not know. These responses are similar to how people respond to change in organizations. There is resistance and confusion along with excitement and anticipation. It's a great opportunity to introduce your child to leading change.

Once you've discussed leading change with two or three projects like the ones we discussed, continue talking about change whenever it fits the situation, whether it's a big change in your work, moving to a new neighborhood or school, or responding to some other new experience in your family. This is like keeping oil in your car, assuring it's well lubricated and reducing friction that wears it out. Keep going back to how people respond to change and why it's so important for leaders to know how to help people embrace new ideas. This type of interaction will keep your child emotionally limber, so she or he can not only respond to personal changes, but also help others, which is at the core of effective leading.

Chapter 37

Ethical Leading

Theme: Teaching ethics in leadership to your child.

In 2001, Enron, one of the fastest growing energy companies in the United States, filed for bankruptcy because of large-scale fraud. Its CEO, Jeffrey Skilling, was later sent to prison for his role in the collapse and the sophisticated scheme to lie and cheat, due to greed. He and several other Enron executives were convicted of numerous crimes. The formula for organizational death is when you combine power with smart people of weak character.

In the United States, over 40% of company thefts are committed by employees, but the greatest thief is when organizational leaders lack ethical standards. Every week, local, regional, and national news stories describe fiascos of leaders who do unethical things that prevent them from continuing as leaders. Because of a leader's influence, their moral and ethical standards make a much greater impact than anyone else's. That's why it is so important for us to make sure our young leaders are solid in both their competencies and their character.

History is littered with horrible stories of leaders who do illegal and unethical actions that hurt people. Someone said, "Power corrupts and absolute power corrupts absolutely." The problem is that leaders must deal with power. Without power, they cease to lead. More traffic accidents take place at intersections than anywhere else. More leadership accidents take place at the intersection of power and character than anywhere else, causing all sorts of damage.

That's one of the main reasons I began KidLead several years ago, because I believed that our best leadership training was given to leaders after they were set in their ways in terms of gaining character and competence. The strategic window for teaching leadership skills is ages 10-13, when cognitions and social-emotional maturity are sufficient but character is still pliable. The older we get, the less malleable we are in terms of our character and ethics. It's not that people can't change, it's just that the return on investment is much lower.

That's why, whether you're a parent or an educator, you have so much potential in shaping culture, especially if your child has a high aptitude for leading. Before I offer a couple of ideas for helping your child make a connection between ethics and leading, let me talk about how important a parent is in developing the character of a child. When I was a boy, my grandfather gave me a job to watch cement that had just been poured at one of his new houses. All I had to do was sit there and make sure no one touched it until it was dry, because if a child or teenager came by to walk on or leave his initials in the sidewalk, it would be there permanently.

Children are wet cement. Significant people in the life of a child leave their mark, often permanently. The standards you uphold in your home and classroom set the sail for the values and behaviors of children. More important than what you say is how you act. In organizational behavior, we describe this as espoused values versus enacted values. Just because a company says it believes in something doesn't mean it actually does it. Your enacted values as a parent are more important than what you espouse, or what you say. Although bad childhood role models don't set up a child for failure, it is interesting that most of the notoriously evil leaders throughout history experienced absent or evil parenting.

Let's talk now about helping your child make a connection between leading and ethics. Here are two ideas.

The first involves paying for a job. Come up with some type of work that your child can do, appropriate to his or her age, for money. It could involve cleaning something, such as a closet or refrigerator, or helping you with a work project. Set an amount of money that you'll pay upon completion. After the project is finished, place only half of the money you said you'd give inside an envelope with your child's name on it. The idea is to let your child open it without you being present, to create more tension in terms of not being paid the amount you offered. If your child is younger, meaning under 10, you'll want to have a conversation the same day, but if your child is 10 or over, you may want to be unavailable until the next day. The reason for the gap between when your child opens the envelope and when you talk is to allow frustration and tension to build. This will create a more potent learning condition.

If your child gets upset before there's sufficient time to build the tension, then postpone your discussion for a while. This may be difficult for you if you're an attentive parent, but don't decrease the impact of the experience. When you talk, explain that this was a lesson. When you say you'll do something but don't keep your word, such as the rate of pay, that is unethical. It's not fair. When leaders do this to people who are on their team, it makes the people angry and causes them not to trust them as much. That's why it's so important for leaders to do what is right, to keep their word, and to treat their team members fairly. Then, after the talk, give your child double the amount that you still owe him, as a reward for receiving the lesson.

Another idea to teach about leadership ethics is to build a house out of paper, while using different standards. This is a variation of one of our activities in KidLead training curriculum. To do this activity, you'll need a pair of scissors, tape, and four or five sheets of copy paper. First, you'll need to create two paper rulers, each with the numbers 1 through 10 evenly spaced. The space between each of the numbers on the first ruler is 1 centimeter. The space between each of the numbers on the other ruler is 1.5 centimeters. Thus, the second ruler will be 50% longer than the first. Don't mention the difference in the rulers.

Hand your child one of the rulers. Then, instruct him to create an open box from a sheet of paper that is 10 units wide by 10 units high by 10 units long. You will build your box using the other ruler. When you finish, you'll both see how different the two boxes are even though you both had the same instructions, a 10x10x10 paper box. If you want to take this a step further, you can put something to eat in each of the boxes and let your child pick which one she wants. If you put something fun to eat in them, no doubt she'll pick the larger one. Then you can talk about the differences in size. Ask questions such as, "Why is one box larger than the other?" "Which box would you want?" And "Are these fair rulers we used?"

The idea is to distinguish the differences between the rulers. They represent ethical standards. A leader who has a smaller ruler or standard than someone else will not lead the same. That's why it's so important for leaders to have high standards, so people trust you and feel like they want to follow you.

When you help your child understand issues related to ethics and leadership, you obviously strengthen a child who's gifted in leadership, but you also show a child not gifted in leading to recognize unethical leaders so that she or he can avoid following them.

Chapter 38

Cultivating Trust

Theme: Teaching your child about integrity in leadership.

In the previous chapter, we discussed teaching ethics in the context of leadership. In this section, we want to go further and focus on integrity. Even though our leadership training curricula at KidLead are designed for ages 3-23, we include integrity as one of the 16 leader qualities because it's so important. If a leader lacks integrity, it may be the most difficult single aspect because it affects everything else. Integrity is the glue that creates trust. Without trust, people will not follow another person. It's the currency of leadership. That's why people who aren't trusted often resort to coercion and fear to make others comply to their demands.

Integrity and ethics are related, but they are different. Ethics has more to do with standards and tends to be more external, how we conduct ourselves. Integrity is more about character and tends to be internal. The English word *integrity* is from the Latin term meaning integer, which means complete, whole. An integer is a whole number, but a fraction is an incomplete number. A person with integrity is whole, meaning she is on the inside what she appears to be on the outside. So literally, you could be a crook and still have integrity if you admitted that you lie and steal, but obviously we're talking about consistency of strong character, not weak or evil character.

When I was a boy, I lived on a farm in Iowa. The winters were very cold there. The pond would freeze over, but before we walked on it, we had to test it to make sure it wouldn't crack. We needed to test its integrity before putting much weight on it, or it might break and we could drown. An important thing for leaders is making sure their actions reflect what they say. In organizational behavior, we call these espoused values versus enacted values. What a company says about itself on its website or in its publicity is what it espouses about itself. But what it actually *does* is its enacted values. We don't trust a company that says it cares for people but then takes advantage of them. The same is true of leaders.

A word related to integrity is sincerity. The word *sincere* comes from the Greek words literally meaning "without wax." In the ancient marketplace, lesser quality clay pots sometimes had cracks in them, so makers would fill in the cracks with wax to make them look perfect. The only way you could see if they were flawed was to hold them to the sun or a bright light. The ones that had no cracks had a sign that said *sin cere*, meaning "no wax." We don't trust a person with large character cracks, and a leader with large character cracks can be dangerous to follow.

So how do you teach this concept to your child? Discussing integrity could be as simple as apologizing when you said you'd do something with her but either forgot or got busy at work. When she says, "But you promised," it's a good time to admit you were wrong and talk about that. Obviously, modeling integrity is important, so work hard to do what you say you'll do.

Here's an activity you might do that illustrates the role of integrity in leadership. I use the word illustrate because it's not a tangible comparison, so for children under 10, you'll need to explain it further since they're more concrete learners and less conceptual. Trust is the glue that sticks followers to a leader. To illustrate this, get craft materials such as paper, colored markers, and scissors. The key is getting two types of adhesives. You'll want to find one that is not very sticky and one that is sticky. You may be able to create a less sticky adhesive if you get a glue stick and let it dry out for a day or two by leaving off its cover. A stickier kind might be a white liquid glue.

Next is suggest to your child that you're putting together a team and you each get to pick two people to be on it. This could be a sports team or school project team or whatever makes sense. Then draw two individual people on paper and cut them out, so you can glue both to a different sheet of paper. Use the sticky glue for one and the not-so-sticky glue for the other. Then post the picture in a place where it can be seen. Soon, or within a day or so, the character with the not-as-sticky glue will fall off. This offers a strong visual illustration as you ask coaching questions such as, "Why did this person fall off our paper?" "Why do you think people choose not to stick to us as leaders?" and "How can we get people to want to follow us?"

A more daring activity that illustrates and builds trust is to do a trust fall. This is where a person folds his arms across his chest and falls backward, trusting that others will not let him hit the ground or get hurt. You can do this with a smaller person standing and a larger, stronger person standing or kneeling behind the person, who then catches the other. It can also be done with the trusting person standing on a table for more height. Obviously, you may need to enlist more people to create a support net by holding each other's arms as you face each other. It needs to be safe, or you'll actually work against the idea of trusting each other. The feeling of falling, trusting others for your safety, is a powerful lesson to experience.

Then ask coaching questions that focus on how a leader's actions affect a person's trust. When you tell someone to fall, you'd better make sure you can catch them. If you don't do what you say, people won't trust you, and your ability to lead will decrease.

Teaching young leaders about the importance of integrity and being trustworthy is important. Yet it's important for all people to understand this so they can decide who they should follow and who they should not follow. Obeying people who say one thing but do another creates problems for those who follow them, their organizations, and eventually an entire culture. Throughout history, leaders lacking integrity have hurt so many. Here's your chance to make history by changing the future.

Chapter 39

Growing Responsible Leaders

Theme: Developing responsibility in your child.

Growing up on a farm taught me responsibility. One of my chores, from age 10 and up, involved cleaning hog stalls for a couple of hours after school. I'd let the sows out of their pens so they could eat while I scooped the manure and wet straw, then lay down fresh, dry straw. I'd push the smelly pile to the end of the barn and with a shovel, lift it into a wagon that would be taken to the field and spread as fertilizer. When the sows had litters, we'd also have to make sure the baby pigs were fed and watered after they finished nursing. The animals needed us to take care of them around the clock, so we did.

The word *responsibility* implies the ability to respond, to act. A responsible person is a dependable person. They show up for work, aren't lazy, display self-discipline, and make sure the job gets done. People depend on them to follow through. Naturally, we want our children to grow up to be responsible people, but leaders need this quality more than everyone else because leaders are responsible for people. When a leader is undependable, we're all sunk. That's why responsibility is one of the 16 characteristics that we include in our KidLead training curriculum. So how can you help your child develop this important quality?

I do not claim to be an expert in child psychology. My wife and I raised three sons who seem to be productive, motivated, and responsible men. But that doesn't make us experts on parenting or teaching responsibility, so I don't want to overstep my bounds here. Our emphasis here is on developing responsibility as a leader. Dependability comes down to learning the discipline of doing what is required when it isn't fun. I teach a graduate class at USC Marshall School of Business called Human Capital Performance and Motivation. It's primarily a course that teaches various theories of motivation. The most powerful way to motivate humans is to reward desired behavior. Let me say that again, it's to reward desired behavior. Too many people try to move people the way we move animals, by driving them, yelling, and occasionally prodding them with a stick. But as a former farmer, I can attest that hogs will also come if you call them. It also helps having a bucket of corn to shake.

My point here is that teaching responsibility is difficult because you're trying to reinforce a behavior that often does not get rewarded in life, at least not quickly. You want your child or children to keep their room clean, brush their teeth, and care for their friends and siblings, not because you're there telling them to, threatening punishment or offering a reward, but because they have learned dependability and to act out of necessity. So how do you do this?

As with most human qualities, we tend to replicate what we see when we're young and impressionable. Including your child in your household chores will model responsibility. Asking your child to move his feet while you run the vacuum around him, while he plays a video game, demonstrates the benefits of having a maid more than it does cleaning his living space. As much as possible, include your kids while you do your chores instead of waiting to do them after they're in bed or at school. That way they don't think there's a fairy who magically folds the laundry and cleans the kitchen, only to wake up as a 23-year-old in an apartment filled with dirty clothes and dishes.

Here are a couple of other ideas to help reinforce the quality of dependability, especially as a leader.

Get a family pet, at least for a period of time, such as two or three months. This pet might be a goldfish, a dog, or even a house plant. That's right, a house plant. The goal is for your child to experience the discipline of feeding and watering, and in the case of a dog, walking and cleaning up after a living thing that depends on your child's care. In the case of the fish or the plant, if it dies, this too becomes an opportunity to discover what happens when we're undependable. Things that rely on us get hurt. While you don't want to make your child feel guilty, a potential punishment versus a reward, you do want to help your child make a connection between doing what is needed by those depending on us to keep them alive and healthy.

A larger activity to practice responsibility is putting your child in charge of an event such as a game night or even a sleepover. If being the boss makes them think they need to be bossy, offer some coaching. The goal is to help your child feel the weight of being in charge and responsible for people having fun. Obviously, depending on the age and maturity levels, the event can be simple or grand, but it should challenge your child.

Planning the event should include a team so it's truly leadership and not just individual effort. Who is going to prepare the food, the invitations, and what's the budget? What is the agenda for the event, meaning what are we going to do when people arrive? Who'll keep the activities going, and what if people don't seem to be having fun or if they have requests? Finally, how is the house going to get cleaned, by whom and when? Each of these items place a sense of burden and responsibility on your child who is in charge. After the event, debrief how things went and applaud your child's responsibility.

Naturally, there's a good chance some things will go wrong or at least change from the original plans, as they typically do in life and leading. Being dependable means that decisions must be made. Doing activities like this, over and over, strengthens the responsibility muscle, growing a self-sufficient individual. But even more important, it develops a dependable leader who takes care of the people she or he leads.

Chapter 40
Growing Grit

Theme: Developing commitment and perseverance in young leaders.

Thomas Edison, the inventor of numerous breakthroughs including the telephone and light bulb, said, "Ninety percent of a person's success is perspiration." Someone else modified that saying which went, "Eighty percent of life is just showing up." Both address the powerful quality of commitment, persevering through difficult times and what has lately been referred to as grit. Even though I am honored to teach at some top tier universities, the bottom line is that IQ, education, and network are secondary if a person lacks the ability to persevere through difficult challenges.

Commitment and persevering are even more important for leaders, because if a leader lacks this quality, then she or he will be unable to inspire others to go through difficult times. A non-committal leader isn't much of a leader at all. Any goal worth achieving will face conditions when there's a temptation to quit, to give up. In his bestselling book *The Dip*, Seth Godin talks about the trough in the s-curve, where nearly any great endeavor or skill hits a low—a difficult time after the initial phase when the desire to give up enters the picture.

History is full of stories where people gave up and failed while those who did not succeeded. Persevering isn't everything, but few things without it ever become anything. Here are some ideas to help you teach this quality to your children.

First, have a talk about perseverance so that you can introduce it to your child. One of the best ways to do this is to tell stories from your life. Chances are, you have experiences where you've persevered and when you've quit. Children love stories. As always, you'll need to modify these according to your child's age and maturity level. But if you can, make them interesting and show emotion. What happened? What were the results? What did you learn from your experience?

The opportunity to share your stories isn't just an opportunity to teach this principle, but also a way to leave a legacy. You never know when a story you share with your child will become one that he or she shares with his or her children. Tribal stories are important parts of leadership. These become anchors that remind your child to persevere in the future when faced with a situation where he or she is tempted to quit and give up.

Next, consider a project that you can design with your child that rewards consistency and commitment. There are a number of options you can develop, but here are a few to get you going.

What would it be like if you rewarded your child for doing a task for an entire month, 30 days in a row? This could be something as simple as brushing teeth before bed or cleaning his room before going to sleep or putting away all of her toys by 7 p.m. Figure out what makes sense to you and then make this deal: you'll only give the prize if your child does the task every day for 30 days in a row.

Naturally, you can negotiate issues such as if you're traveling or perhaps offering a one-time exception, or whatever makes sense, but make sure you do this in advance because it will be easy for you to give in if the going gets tough. In other words, if you compromise on the deal and fail to follow through, you'll be doing what you don't want to do. I know that we've emphasized how leadership involves other people, but tenacity and persevering is often seen as an individual quality of leaders, in addition to their commitment as leader. In other words, until you've developed it as an individual, it will be very difficult to convey it as a leader.

The reason is that one of the biggest effects of a leader's individual commitment is how it inspires followers to do the same. When team members see the leader persevering and sacrificing in the pursuit of a goal, they are more likely to do the same. Remember, leaders are thermostats, not thermometers. Thermometers tell the temperature, but thermostats set the temperature.

Another idea to teach this to your child is to spontaneously reward your child in situations where you see her demonstrating commitment despite difficult conditions. This can be any number of situations, whether it's committing to learning a musical instrument or sport, or following through on a difficult school topic, or even sticking with a friend who is causing conflict and unnecessary drama. Being aware of situations where your child is enduring difficult conditions and then acknowledging them is a powerful way you can teach commitment as well as reward the desired behavior. Naturally, you don't want to reward everything so that you make it easy, but you do want to help them understand why persevering is so valuable.

One of the interesting discoveries over the last few years is identifying what is commonly known as mirror neurons in our brains. They are behind the reason we're prone to smile when we see a baby smiling, or tear up when we see others crying, or when we feel pensive or anxious when we see another person in distress. Therefore, it is vital that a leader convey commitment and dedication, because others cannot help but take their cues from them. If a leader waffles, others will as well. Followers tend to mimic what they see.

Well-meaning parents often confuse love with making it easy for their children, with the unfortunate result of hindering their ability to fly on their own. Helping young leaders learn commitment and perseverance is a vital part of their development.

Chapter 41

The Secret of People

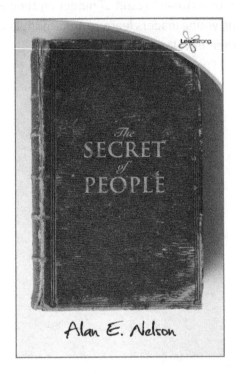

Theme: Teaching young leaders the value of honoring others; *The Secret of People.*

When my wife and I were newly married, we were driving one day, heading into Los Angeles. I keep up with traffic, but apparently the person behind me didn't think I was going fast enough. He passed me and as he did, made a hand gesture which in our culture let me know he didn't think much of me. That made me angry, and I was about to say something when my wife calmly said, "That guy's not having a very good day, is he?" I didn't say anything, but her comment made me realize, "She's right. His impatience reflected more what was going on inside of him than it did me."

That idea of reading what's going on inside of people via their behaviors became a book I authored called *The Secret of People*. Although it sounds precocious, claiming to know the secret of people, I'm convinced of it. If you study the wars and social conflicts throughout history, you'll find this principle at the root of them all. It's the reason your kids fight with each other, people get their feelings hurt, and husbands and wives divorce. This issue is also fundamental to what we love and what we loathe about leaders.

The secret of people is that everyone you'll ever meet is interested primarily in one thing: being valued. Honor is treating another person with dignity, recognizing their individual worth. Regardless of ethnicity, politics, ideologies, income, gender, age, or religion, people want to feel respected. Regardless of what you base this universal need for honor upon, it's very tangible. When a driver cuts someone off, the person offended gets angry because of the other driver's failure to honor him. When a child hits a sibling for taking her toy, she does it as a response to feeling disrespected. When a country doesn't honor the other's boundaries, it is attacked by the other's military.

While it may seem like an over-simplification, feeling dishonored is at the root of most relationship problems. People desire dignity from others. Because leadership is a social construct, leaders need to understand this principle. If they lack strong social skills, they'll have problems, resulting in a reduced ability to lead.

To honor another person is to recognize her value, to treat her with dignity. Honor is not so much an emotion like infatuation and love. Rather, it is about attitude and action. Opportunities to recognize the value in others are all around us, whether we're getting the door for another person or complimenting them on what they're wearing or giving them the right of way at an intersection. Every person asks a silent question: "Do you recognize my value and will you honor me for it?" If you respond correctly, you'll do well. If you do not, you'll have problems.

What does this have to do with your child? Regardless of an inclination to lead, she or he will benefit from intentionally using the secret of people. If your child has a strong aptitude for leading, it will become an invaluable skill. Here are three ideas to help teach this principle to your child.

First, begin with something simple, such as writing thank-you notes to four or five people in your child's network. This might be a teacher, coach, tutor, friend, or a parent of a friend. Come up with a list of people, and then help your child brainstorm things that he or she appreciates about this person. If possible, try to make the comments specific. For example, if she's writing to a teacher, avoid saying "Thank you for being a great teacher." Rather, express something such as "Thank you for the time you take to help me understand my math. I also notice how patient you are when the other students are talking and being loud." Research shows that people value more specific affirmations than generic ones. You may want to purchase some nice-looking "thank you" notes to make it more official and add more value. On the other hand, perhaps homemade notes that your child creates would be perceived as more special.

Another way to teach this skill is to practice this principle around your home. Talk about the idea of honoring each other, whether it's in the context of resolving a conflict between siblings or giving dignity in terms of how you respond to one another. You could think of ideas to offer respect as a special gift. The latter could take the form of writing appreciation notes for each other, such as making smiley faces on Post-it notes and then putting them around the house. The goal of this is not just to encourage each other as family members, but also to get used to the practice of communicating honor and dignity to people in general. Teaching your child to say "thank you" to check-out clerks at the store, say "have a nice day" to the server at the restaurant, or express gratitude to people who serve your family through the course of a week is important. Gratitude is a form of honoring others for what they do for us.

Finally, honoring seems most difficult when we feel we've been dishonored. Here's how a conversation might go in the context of sibling rivalry. Let's say that your two kids, or your child and a friend, are upset with each other about the use of a toy. It may go something like this:

"Jill, I can tell you're upset that Sophia played with your toy without asking you."

Jill says, "Yes, I told her not to touch my stuff."

You respond, "Did you feel that Sophia wasn't respecting you because she did that?"

She says, "Yes, I've told her several times that she needs to ask me first."

You respond, "I understand that. We all want to be honored for our requests, don't we?"

"Yes."

"Okay, good," you respond. "What would be a way that you could tell her your feelings without dishonoring her?"

"What do you mean?"

"I mean, you're mad because you feel like Sophia didn't honor you by playing with your toy without asking. I'm asking, how can you let her know you're upset without disrespecting her?"

"Well, I guess I could say 'Sophia, next time, if you want to play with my things, please ask me first.'"

"That's awesome," you say. "I think if you say it that way, you will let her know that you're upset, but you're doing it in a way that honors her."

The more you practice conversations like this, the better your children will get at understanding what honor sounds like. While it seems simple, it is one of the most powerful principles for improving relationships. Imagine what it would be like if our national leaders did this with each other. Our world would be a far better place.

- *The Secret of People* is a book by Alan E. Nelson, available on Amazon.com

Chapter 42

Confidence Building

Theme: How to help your child become a more confident leader.

Parents want their children to be confident as people, but this quality is essential for leading. Leaders who don't convey courage and confidence in the face of difficult circumstances don't get followed. As someone said, "He who thinks he is leading, when no one is following, is merely taking a walk." Let me compare and contrast two important terms, *confidence* and *courage*. Granted, these are quite different, and yet in the context of leadership, they're similar in how they impact would-be followers.

Courage is the internal fortitude to face difficult situations. It's not a lack of fear, but rather a willingness and ability to transcend fears. Some of the most courageous people are those with fear who don't allow it to hold them back. Conversely, sometimes people without fear are applauded for their courage, which can also be dangerous. But usually, people who appear to be courageous are actually confident, in that they're able to keep their fear under control because they're competent and familiar with the situation. My friend, who is a retired Navy fighter pilot and Top Gun instructor, has done more harrowing things than I can ever imagine doing. At the same time, he would be one of the first to admit that much of his extreme abilities came from years of training and experience in taking off and landing on aircraft carriers, launching missiles, and flying at high speeds.

A person who seems confident without ability or experience is dangerous. Being aloof to risks is a sign of immaturity and foolishness. What's the first key to developing confident kids? Begin with the end in mind. What do you want your child to become? For example, if you want your child to become a confident leader, then start offering opportunities to lead small teams of people in small projects at an early age. That's why we created KidLead, so that kids as young as 3 can start experiencing leading organizationally. Not many 10-year-olds in the world get executive skill training, but KidLead offers that. If you want your child to be a strong communicator, then begin having him or her present formal speeches in front of you and others. The more familiar we become with something, anything, the less fear we'll feel and the more confident we'll be. Think of when you moved to a new home or began a new job. After a year or so, you were very comfortable with your surroundings and behaviors, primarily because of familiarity. Comfort and confidence are siblings. Comfort is created with familiarity.

Another way to develop confident and courageous children is to increase their self-efficacy. This is a term that refers to a person's perception of what he can achieve. The good news is that self-efficacy can be learned. Most of my university students in the last 20 years are identified as the millennial generation. While some people write disparaging things about members of this generation, one thing for sure is that many have high self-efficacy. They have the sense that they can achieve a lot.

One reason for this is that many of their parents invested heavily in their lives, whether it be in sports, after-school tutoring, arts, or personal growth programs. Chances are if you're reading this, you're that kind of parent, so keep it up.

At the same time, beware the Tiger Mom syndrome—the parent who places inordinate pressure on a child that results in kids who lose their childhood because of driven parents living out their lost dreams through their kids. Each child is different, but regardless of personality, each can gain self-esteem and self-efficacy. Self-esteem is being valued for who you are. Self-efficacy is believing in what you can do. The danger is building self-esteem on what you can do, because failing will result in hopelessness and depression.

While developing KidLead, we lived in Monterey, California. I did some work in nearby Salinas, where a lot of the produce in the U.S. is grown. Many of the residents work in the fields. A number of families there weren't interested in having their children in our leadership program, because they viewed it as a waste of time. They said, "Our kids will have a boss, but they won't be a boss." This thinking was an extension of their own self-perception, not based on a realistic assessment of their children. For a year I taught at a community college there, where over 80% of the students were the first ones to ever attend college. Breaking free of low self-efficacy in a family is not easy, but it is possible.

Here's my point: continually strive to elevate your child's sense of achievement, not in a pressure to perform manner, but via an array of experiences. This helps your child discover what he or she enjoys and is good at doing. Usually these go hand in hand. Organizational behavior research shows that there's a stronger correlation between a person performing well and being satisfied than there is in trying to improve job satisfaction for better performance. We tend to like what we're good at, so set up your child for success. Help them put wins under their belt. Once you find something your child enjoys and seems to have a natural talent in, take it to the next level and don't waste time or money doing other things. Positive psychology shows that we're more apt to be successful in life by leveraging our strengths versus working on our weaknesses. Proficiency elevates confidence and overflows into other areas. A soccer star will be a more confident software employee.

Help your child face his or her fears gradually, beginning with baby steps. Think of it as walking. Walking is basically the process of falling forward. We lean forward, move our foot, and then lean forward again and move our other foot. Whether it's walking, riding a bicycle, or taking off from an aircraft carrier in a fighter jet, they all begin with small steps. Don't just assume your kids are gaining confidence; help them. Yet sometimes the best help you can provide is taking away your hands, rather than hovering over them so they don't have to face their fears. This is the stuff of self-efficacy, learning to achieve things on our own.

Growing confident and courageous leaders is at the heart of KidLead, by giving them a huge head start. Why wait until middle adulthood before we begin executive skill training? Why not begin early so that by the time they become adults, they're leading from a comfort zone?
Even if your child isn't preconditioned to lead, you can help him or her become a great team member, a person who great leaders will want on their team. Growing a great adult is your job. Well done, reading this book. But don't be disappointed if you don't see immediate results. I live in the city of Thousand Oaks. It gets its name from the many oak trees surrounding us. Each of these great trees began as a tiny acorn. When you look at your child, don't see an infant or 5-year-old or preteen. You're growing a confident oak.

Chapter 43

Developing Humble Leaders

Theme: Helping your child become a servant leader.

Throughout history, the leaders we respect the most and desire to emulate are those who convey the quality of humility. That's why we made this quality one of the 16 characteristics in our KidLead curriculum. Unfortunately, humility is often misunderstood and has a lack of role models. The traditional model of a leader is a person who is larger than life, occupies a giant office, drives a fancy car, and is wealthy, demanding, and aloof. This person takes advantage of others, so while we often have a disdain for this person, we also admire them and envy them.

In reality, the role of the leader is to serve people. The fact that leaders often get paid more than others is because of their unique ability to bring out the best in people, to help us accomplish together what we would not or could not as individuals. Unfortunately, power often goes to people's heads and brings out the worst qualities of human nature. Therefore, many leaders are self-centered, power-hungry, and committed to their own success and achievement. This is unfortunate, because leading is about serving. Think of humility as a weight to counterbalance power, which is required for leading. Without it, pride and narcissism will result.

In our KidLead curriculum, we generally use the terms *servanthood* and *servant leader* as a way to communicate the element of humility. In some cultures, such as the Middle East, servanthood is not something to be emulated, so there we use the term "humility." The word in English is an interesting term. Its etymology shares the root of the word "humus," referring to rich, fertile soil. As I've mentioned, I grew up on a farm. Part of our land was next to a river. Every spring it flooded, bringing all sorts of topsoil and elements such as dead plants and animals that fertilized the dirt. This was what we called Grade-A soil. It grew the best crops.

My point is that humility is a fertile character soil that produces great results. Leaders who lack humility are not nearly as effective as those who have it, who are loved and respected by their followers. Therefore, if your child has leadership aptitude, it's imperative for you to help your child think of leading as a way to serve others, not as an excuse to be bossy and take advantage of other people.

Here's the challenge: leading involves power, so humble leaders and servant leaders need to be able to handle power responsibly and not let it go to their heads, making them think they're better than others. The role of the leader is simply a team role, yet it's more important because it involves everyone else, helping team members bring out their strengths. The leader is often not the smartest or the most talented person on the team. Rather, the leader is usually the most skilled in helping people work together as a team. This is a powerful ability, typically resulting in higher pay and more benefits. But when these things make the leader proud, they diminish the leader's ability.

Therefore, your role as a parent is to help your child be humble, whether as a leader or a team member. This single quality in both roles is fundamental to being teachable, endearing, and thus effective. Here are three simple ideas of how to do this.

1. *Teach gratitude.* We've talked about this before, but gratitude is the sibling of humility. The science of human behavior teaches us that one of the best ways to develop a certain attitude is to do behaviors that foster it. For example, if you want to help your child develop an attitude of charity and concern for the poor, it's more effective to take your child to a charity that feeds the homeless than it is to merely talk about being grateful or caring for the poor. Many charities welcome volunteers to help them care for the poor and hungry. Find an agency near you and then volunteer to serve along with your child. This type of experience does two things. It models servanthood as a parent, and it offers first-hand opportunities for your child to interact with people who possess fewer opportunities in life. Gratitude can also be taught in writing thank-you notes and expressing appreciation to people who are often overlooked, such as janitors, cooks and food servers, caregivers, and house cleaners. Why not tape a thank-you note to the lid of the garbage can, so the waste management person will see it?

2. *Reward humility.* Where you see your child letting others go first and acting humbly, reinforce it. Children by nature tend to be self-centered. It's initially a part of survival, looking out for ourselves. Yet as a child matures, he or she needs to think less of themselves and more of others. You can see this in the challenge young children have in sharing their toys, attention, and even food at mealtimes. When you see a child looking out for others, make sure you affirm that. "Jill, I was so impressed when you shared your toy with your little brother. That's

such a neat thing you did." End your comment with a hug and perhaps a food treat. Remember, the strongest motivator of human nature is to reward desired behavior. Catch them doing something well and then pay attention to it and reward it. An option of this is to make a game out of random acts of kindness, where each family member reports a good deed done for someone who can't reward them, such as a stranger or a peer or someone with less power or money. You could even make a plate of cookies and drop it off at a neighbor's house or pick up trash on the ground when you're out for a walk.

3. *Model humility.* Our children are influenced by our behaviors more than our words. Complimenting people who serve you and talking about work situations where you express gratitude to your boss, your colleagues, and team members serve as powerful demonstrations of behaviors that reflect humility. It's quite difficult to talk about humility when you fail to model it as a parent. If you brag, take credit for teamwork, and speak down to people in everyday life such as caregivers, food servers, or others who serve you, chances are your child will learn to mimic your attitude and actions. Often, kids aren't aware of our lives outside of our role as parent. Let your child know about ways that you serve others. It's more about modeling than bragging. If you're not involved in charitable work, get involved. Say "thanks" and demonstrate appreciation for those who serve you. Make sure you are respectful to your spouse, verbally and physically. Don't underestimate the power of role modeling humility.

Although we've focused primarily on the individual trait of humility as opposed to leadership, this is one of the characteristics of a leader that comes down to who the leader is as an individual. Rarely will you ever see a leader who conveys servanthood while being self-centered and proud as an individual. Robert Greenleaf, the author of the bestselling book *Servant Leadership*, wrote, "A servant leader must first become a servant." You can serve without leading, but a servant leader must be both humble and a leader. This is a rare combination that usually requires early modeling and training to be accomplished.

Chapter 44

Developing Optimistic Leaders

Theme: How to grow hope in your children.

Napoleon said, "Leaders are dealers in hope." People thrive on hope. They shrink when they feel despair. That's why leaders who are effective are good at helping people feel excited about the future. There's nothing as important as a leader who encourages followers when things get difficult. The role of a leader is to fan the flames of inspiration, courage, and motivation.

One of my favorite books growing up was *The Power of Positive Thinking* by Norman Vincent Peale. I appreciated that book as a young adult because it inspired me to think positively about life and the challenges I faced. Three other great books like these are *The Magic of Thinking Big* by David Schwartz, *Tough Times Never Last, But Tough People Do!* by Robert Schuller, and *How to Win Friends and Influence People* by Dale Carnegie. These are great books to recommend to your children, when they're ready.

The reason that an optimistic outlook is so important is that people respond to their *perception* of reality, not reality itself. Let me give you an example. Let's say you come home from work one night. Your home is dark. As you walk through the door, you see a movement in the corner of the room. Automatically, your body responds to a potential intruder, a threat. Adrenaline flows through your system and you strike your best martial arts pose, ready to defend yourself against a threat. You flip on the light, only to realize there isn't anything there; it's a false alarm. Reality is that there was never a threat, but your idea that there was created a physiological response for fight or flight.

Optimism and persevering may be the two most powerful characteristics of success in life. They are opposite sides of the same coin of emotional resilience, handling life's ups and downs. We are far less likely to persevere through difficult times without optimism, hope for the future. Pessimism, a perception that things are not going to get better, usually leads to giving up. Although false hope is a reality that causes some people to continue, whether it's with a job, a significant other, or a business, rarely is anything great ever accomplished without an attitude of optimism, a better tomorrow.

Here are three ideas of how you can develop optimism in your child.

First, when your child goes through a challenging situation, brainstorm reasons to be hopeful. Let's say that he doesn't get an A on a school project or get selected to a competitive basketball team. Take out a sheet of paper and come up with at least five positive options related to the outcome. You can begin the process by suggesting things such as:

- What were three things you did well?
- You now have a better idea of what is needed next time.
- You can put your time and energy toward another skill or project.
- You can find out more about this topic on the internet and watch videos.
- You can develop an improvement plan. What might be next?

All of these are opportunities to focus on a preferred future, which is the theme of hope.

Helping people embrace hope is what makes leaders effective. Those who are pessimistic, negative, and create fear and trepidation are never as influential. The reason is that people naturally yearn to hope. They desire to pursue a better life.

In my work with new managers, it's what I teach about the difference between being a boss and being a leader. Bosses often have a negative reputation for focusing on problems and telling people what they're doing wrong. But leaders focus on solutions and helping people use their strengths. An effective leader brings out the best in others. Sometimes you need both, but problems without solutions lead to despair and are demotivating.

A second idea is to make hope visual. This could be a poster or a paper chain. Cut out slips of white paper and get colored markers and some tape. On each slip of paper, write one thing that makes you happy or hopeful. Loop several of these to make a chain. Hang it in your house. Every week, add two to three more links. This visual helps us remember good things and count our blessings. Another idea is to draw and write things that make us happy and hopeful on a poster or flip chart paper. These can include things you're thankful for or goals and hopes you're anticipating, whether it's a family vacation, a new furniture item, or tickets to see your favorite play or sports team. Much of the joy we get from a vacation isn't just the trip; it's the anticipation leading up to the trip. Hope is a positive emotion we get when we anticipate something good. You can hang the flip chart paper or poster in a place where it's out of sight from guests but where the family can see it regularly. Talk about it once a week.

Third, demonstrate hope in your family conversations. Life is filled with challenges. When these occur, how you face them has a lot to do with how your children see life. Focusing on the positive, the good things, and keeping hope alive are all role model responsibilities. That's why two people can look at the same set of circumstances and one responds with despair and gloom and the other with hope and gratitude. We pick our attitudes much like we pick our friends or pick the clothes we wear each day. Empowering children to know this is a responsibility of parents. If you complain about the service in a restaurant or how your boss treats you or the way your child keeps her room, you're conveying negativity. Yet if you express thanks to the waiter, appreciation for your work challenges, and compliment what your child is doing well, you're modeling a hope-filled attitude.

As a parent, your primary strength in fostering this quality in your children is to model it yourself. When you run into difficulties, share this with your children, but focus on the good that can come from it and the positive possibilities. Retaining a positive spirit amidst difficult circumstances is a great way to nurture this attitude in your kids.

As a parent or educator, you've been given one of the biggest opportunities and responsibilities in shaping the life of a child and future leader. You possess the power to help children see what can be, not settle for what is. The best parents and mentors are those who inspire us to pursue our dreams, to accomplish what others say is improbable, if not impossible. While optimism and hope do not guarantee success, pessimism and negativity are recipes for failure. Whether you think you can or you think you can't, you're right. Leaders engage us with the idea of a future that is better than the present. Your ability to influence those who can enable others to pursue the best is powerful. Make the most of it.

Thank you for allowing me to intersect with your life. I am confident that you'll make the world a better place by growing a great adult and investing in a future leader today. Following are some resources that can help you expand on this book and develop your child's leadership potential.

Conclusion

Commencement Vs. Graduation

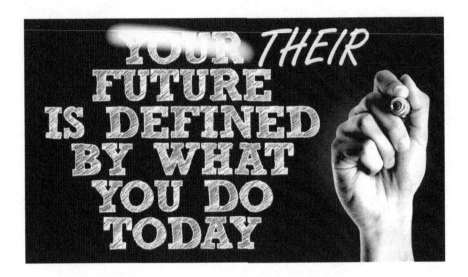

As a higher ed instructor, I get to experience the pomp and circumstance of graduation ceremonies. Donning academic regalia, I march in with other faculty members. Then from the platform, I watch student after student, walk across the stage to receive their diplomas. It's a heart-touching event for all. The interesting thing is that these sacred celebrations are not called graduations. They're referred to as commencements. Graduating is when you complete something. Commencing is when you're starting. Although you're finishing this book, my hope is you'll start taking the leadership development of your child or children seriously. My hunch is that you've already commenced or else you wouldn't have made it this far.

Whether your child is a high, medium or low octane leader, kudos to you for developing his or her potential. Peter Drucker, the father of modern management said, "The best way to predict the future is to create it." By focusing on leaders while they're moldable, not moldy, we stand the best chance of shaping tomorrow today. Never under-estimate the importance of consistent, small actions.

I write these final words as a man in his early 60s. I'm striving to lose some weight, created by a lazy metabolism, in part because my doctor said I'm prehypertensive. I occasionally send our three sons pictures of me in my 20s and 30s, when I looked svelte, as they do now.

Call me an overachiever, but this year I even purchased our burial plots. The now quiet house is filled with photos of our children as toddlers, elementary students, and teens. The noise of laughter and chaos is a faint memory, as I recall the scenes. Now they're grown men with careers. My dad used to say, "Life is like a roll of toilet paper. The less you have left, the faster it goes." That may seem like an odd metaphor, but it's pretty true. Time goes fast. Make the most of the moments you have with your children. It'll be over in a blink. If your children's future was defined by what you did today, who would they turn out to be? My hope is that they'll lead, because the world desperately needs more who do this well.

If you want to change the world,

Focus on leaders.

If you want to change leaders,

Focus on them when they're young.

- Alan E. Nelson

About the Author

 Alan E. Nelson is a leader, professor, and social entrepreneur. Most of his life he's led. After earning a doctorate in leadership from the University of San Diego, he began writing and teaching other leaders. Then at midlife he changed gears, focusing on identifying and developing leaders while they're most pliable, between the ages of 3 and 23. He's the founder of KidLead Inc. (non-profit) and LeadYoung Training Systems, making an impact internationally.

Alan teaches leadership, organizational behavior, and human capital performance and motivation courses at USC Marshall School of Business, the Naval Postgraduate School, and the University of California Irvine's Merage School of Business. He's the author of over 20 books and 100s of articles and podcasts, and he has designed an array of young leader training curricula.

Married to Nancy for over 38 years, the Nelsons have three grown sons and two wonderful granddaughters. They live in Thousand Oaks, California, just north of Los Angeles.

For more info on Alan and his speaking, go to www.AlanENelson.com or via LinkedIn. He's available for training on this book and related leadership topics. For info on his young leader resources, go to www.LeadYoungTraining.com.

Other books by Dr. Nelson:

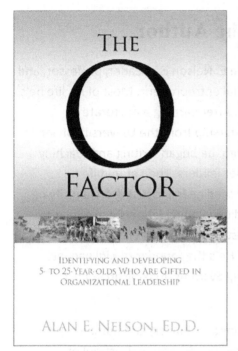

The O Factor represents a significant amount of Dr. Nelson's research and work with emerging leaders internatinoally, between the ages of 3-23. In it he looks at the role of genetics and ways to identify future leaders by observing behaviors in social settings. In addition, there are an array of practical suggestions for developing children, preteens and teens as leaders, designed for parents, educators and those who work with youth.

Although similar in content to My Kid Leads!, this book is a great read for educators, those who work with children and youth in organizations, and for parents desiring a bit deeper look into those possessing a predisposition to organize others, the O Factor. By influencing the influencers, we can leverage our resources on leadership while they're moldable, not moldy.

Available on Amazon.com

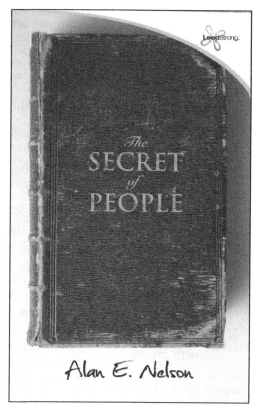

In this engaging, fun-to-read narrative, Alan focuses on how to target the most important single relationship key: treating people with honor. When people behave in a dishonoring manner, it's usually an indicator of what's going on inside of them, not so much a reflection of others. Instead of reacting negatively, we can refocus our attention to address their real need, a desire to be valued.

The narrative takes place in various coffee shops in Monterey and Carmel, California, as the author interacts with a peculiar sage named Paul. It's an engaging story, but all the while explaining some of the most practical ideas to help you succeed in your relationships.

Available on Amazon.com

In this short, easy-to-read book, Dr. Nelson communicates very practical ways to make a difference in the lives of those we meet on a daily basis. In an intriguing story line, similar in style to *The Secret of People*, the author engages with a sage "tourist" visiting Malibu. The conversations and mysterious meetings result in discovering powerful insights for influencing others in five minutes or less. By recognizing these fertile, open windows, we can sow seeds of hope that in turn fulfill us as well. The busyness of life need not limit the impact we make with others.

This is a great book for families, organizations, and individuals who want to take advantage of increasing their impact in short bites.

Available on Amazon.com

Some of the most overlooked resources for leaders are handy tools for training others how to lead. This is not so much a book as it is a training manual, providing leaders and managers with 50 leadership lessons covering an array of sub-topics. Forty-five of the lessons include a 1-page handout (8x11 format) that can be copied for team members. There's also a 1-page Trainer section with suggestions on how to use the lesson, whether you have 5 or 35 minutes. The variety of topics allows you to select the ones that fit your situation, helping you train your team.

The final five lessons are discussion guides for movies with leadership themes. These make fun team-building opportunities but with a purpose. Various aspects of leading can be coached out via strategic questions, offered in the lessons.

Available on Amazon.com

People don't quit jobs, they quit bosses. It's the number one reason exit-seekers give for leaving employment. Gallup research shows that managers are the single most important element of why companies thrive or not. There's a lot riding on being effective as a boss. In The Five-Star Boss, Alan E. Nelson shows you under the hood of organizations, what you need to know when you oversee a team, facility, or division. These short, quick-read chapters allow you to jump around, gleaning content from the author's popular classes at highly ranked business schools.

Over half of new bosses wash out within the first year, primarily because we promote individuals based on their technical skills. But leading people is a whole different mindset, for which few are ever trained. This book is conversational in tone and practical in content. It's a go-to resource for the newbie boss as well as the veteran wanting to brush up on his or her game.

Available on Amazon.com

My Kid Leads!

Made in the USA
Middletown, DE
01 December 2024

65321531R00117